Praise for

ALL IS NOT LOST

"A highly entertaining, intimate, and honest account of a woman's life at a crossroads, told against the psychological backdrop of Hollywood's demands and a young girl's dreams. Shannon has written a beautiful book all women will find themselves in. It is a great read."

—KERRY EHRIN, screenwriter; producer; Emmy, Writers Guild, and Women's Image Network Award nominee—*Friday Night Lights, Parenthood, Bates Motel,* and *The Morning Show*

"Such an incredibly brave, raw, and beautiful book! *All Is Not LOST* is a story about Shannon's readjustment from the life she thought she'd be living to the one she actually is. Her honesty is almost uncomfortable at times as she identifies so many truths that I also see in myself but that I daren't express. This is a must-read that will also satisfy your wanderlust, as Shannon captures the beauty of Hawaii and the profound way this place can touch you like no other."

—HENRY IAN CUSICK, actor, writer, director—Desmond Hume on *LOST* (Emmy nomination), Stephen Finch on *Scandal*, Marcus Kane on *The 100*, Russell Taylor on *MacGyver*

"Shannon's touching, chucklesome, and shoot-from-the-ovaries testimony reminds me that those obligatory ruts in life—be it bereavement, heartbreak, or 'stuckness'—are things that are happening *for* me, not *to* me. How do we unleash the energy to move ahead of our creative dead ends? How do we overcome the unseen forces that stand in the way of inspiration? Read this gorgeous narrative. You just may give yourself the confidence and permission to move past your feeling of being stuck."

—VERA FARMIGA, actress; director; producer; Academy Award, Emmy, BAFTA, Golden Globe, Screen Actors Guild, Critics Choice, Independent Spirit nominee—TV shows: *Bates Motel, When They See Us*—Films: *Up In the Air, The Departed, The Conjuring* Franchise, *The Front Runner*

"Carbonell manages to make her uncommon experience—relocating her family to paradise where her husband is acting on the beloved series, *LOST*—into a wholly relatable and poignant memoir about family, self-sacrifice, and the desperate need for solitude, despite feeling alone. Reading her story is like having wine with girlfriends and upon leaving, feeling elated and fiercely loving everything you have, including the friendships that made the recognition possible."

—KAUI HART HEMMINGS, American author of *The Descendants, The Possibilities,* and *How to Party with an Infant*

ALL
IS
NOT
LOST

ALL

IS

NOT

LOST

HOW I FRIENDED FAILURE ON
THE ISLAND AND FOUND A WAY HOME

SHANNON KENNY CARBONELL

GREENLEAF
BOOK GROUP PRESS

Published by Greenleaf Book Group Press
Austin, Texas
www.gbgpress.com

Distributed by Greenleaf Book Group

For ordering information or special discounts for bulk purchases, please contact Greenleaf Book Group at PO Box 91869, Austin, TX 78709, 512.891.6100.

Design and composition by Greenleaf Book Group
Cover design by Greenleaf Book Group
Cover Image: ©iStockphoto.com/Jag_cz

Publisher's Cataloging-in-Publication data is available.

Print ISBN: 978-1-62634-767-0

eBook ISBN: 978-1-62634-768-7

Part of the Tree Neutral® program, which offsets the number of trees consumed in the production and printing of this book by taking proactive steps, such as planting trees in direct proportion to the number of trees used: www.treeneutral.com

TreeNeutral®

Printed in the United States of America on acid-free paper

21 22 23 24 25 26   10 9 8 7 6 5 4 3 2 1

First Edition

For Nestor, who always holds the door open for me without fail.

And for Mum and Dad, who gave me unspoken license to walk on through.

Prologue

JANUARY 2010

"I can't do the red carpet with you," I whispered to Nestor once we settled into the town car. "I'm just . . . ugh. I feel fat and ugly. I don't want to be photographed."

"You look beautiful," he said, a little too loudly.

"Shhh. Please," I begged. I didn't want the driver to hear us. And then the tears came.

I tilted my head back and breathed deeply, hoping to stem the tide. My fake lashes had taken so damn long to apply. I couldn't risk ruining them.

Nestor did as I asked: He let it go.

I kept my head back, just in case. "I'm sorry," I whispered.

He shrugged. "It's not a big deal. I don't care about any of this stuff."

It was true. He didn't care about attention from the press or the public's perception of him. Walking the red carpet for the premiere episode of the final season of *LOST* was merely a part of his job. But I also knew he'd be happier with me by his side while he courted his fans and the media. The problem was, I *did* care about all that stuff.

All my life I'd wanted to be a Famous Actress. Not *just* an actress. I'd always been desperate to be *seen*, to be *known*. Yet now I didn't want anyone to recognize me, to survey what I'd become: an actress who had given up on her career and on maintaining her size 6 body.

But how can an invisible person be famous? It's been said that fame only exists quantitatively—there is the star, and there are the star's many fans. That's all there is to it. And no matter how shallow the equation of fame proved to be, I'd programmed myself to want it. So now I had a big problem: If I was noticed—noticed by large numbers of people—I existed. If I was not . . .

Hiding wasn't simply hiding. Hiding was wiping out the equation. Hiding was erasing myself.

I apologized to Nestor again. He told me not to sweat it—again.

Once we stepped out of the car, the crowd of onlookers began calling out his name, each voice begging him to come and talk. Photographers surrounded him. The cacophony of calls, camera clicks, and the baseline buzz of chatter jolted me out of my ruminative stupor. I watched Nestor pleasing both fans and the media as he moved down the red carpet. Then I lost sight of him in the press of the crowd and the bleached fog of sea spray, sand dust, and camera flashes. He entered the land of flawless men and women spun into gods and goddesses. And I was stranded, left behind, a mortal who was forever barred from the kingdom.

I snuck away to a little tented area to wait with the other partners who didn't want to walk the red carpet. We made small talk for a while, until suddenly the crowd gave a huge roar. I looked out from under the tent.

A Famous Actress had arrived.

Evangeline Lilly—Evie, as the cast called her—played Kate, the female lead. I thought she was excellent in her role, but I had no idea who she really was as a person. Nestor rarely worked on set with her, and she mistakenly called him Chester. He didn't have the heart to correct her the first time, so he'd let it go until it had reached the point of no return.

She looked just like I'd always wanted to look—petite and soft. Her skin was flushed and glistening as she beamed at the people and the press. She smiled with her eyes—they crinkled and danced about as she moved through the crowd. When she lifted her slender, perfectly sculpted arm and waved, I could feel the sweat dripping down my own inner arm flab and my back-fat-minimizing bra. *She* had an outside I'd be glad to share with the world.

She had what I wanted.

When the fans looked at her, they probably felt they knew her. What they saw was a happy, sweet, effortless beauty who'd been blessed with talent and deserved great fortune. She was entrancing. I couldn't take my eyes off her. I sighed deeply, seeing her just as the crowd did.

I wanted to be her.

I wanted all that adoration and unconditional love heaped upon me by strangers.

I knew I had big love, true love, real love, right in front of me, three times over: one husband and two little boys. But the number felt too small. I craved quantity, not quality. Three was not thousands. Three was not millions.

The reality is, no young woman goes to Hollywood with the dream of becoming a wife and a mom. I had failed.

And so I wanted to be erased.

Chapter One

JANUARY 2006

The time had come to give up acting.

I drove west through Los Angeles, my hands sweating, my heavy heart beating fast through my bra. I was on my way to my manager's office in Pacific Palisades to tell her I was quitting. The light, the glow, the fame—it had all eluded me. I was finally going to admit defeat.

As I traveled down Interstate 10, an image flew up from my memory and flashed through my mind—words written in my mother's red nail polish across a torn page of newspaper:

SHANNON KENNY WILL BE A

FAMOUS ACTRESS

I'd painted those words in a frenzied scrawl when I was twelve years old, on the only piece of parchment I could find. It was my own strange, solo, preteen commitment ceremony.

I'd just finished dancing that day, and I remember the dance well because my moves were always the same: I'd spin around frantically and then tuck myself into a little ball like an ice skater. After a beat or two, I'd explode out of the ball and undulate my spine as I threw my head about recklessly. But on that day, at the end of my dance, I turned off my cassette player and wrote my vow.

SHANNON KENNY WILL BE A
FAMOUS ACTRESS

The vow was everything: to be special, to be singled out, to be seen as separate from the rest. I believed if I were able to live under that kind of golden light when I grew up, I'd be happy. But I was just as sure that if anyone found out I'd made that vow, I'd be excoriated for my arrogance.

So upon committing my promise to paper, I folded it over and over again, into a tiny flat square, and shoved it into a white cardboard box. I wrote the word "private" on the box and opened the wooden hope chest at the end of my bed.

The top of the walnut chest was covered with faux quilted leather, the exact color of French's Classic Yellow Mustard. I maneuvered my arm through an elbow-deep jumble of toys and old schoolbooks until I found a back corner in which to place the box. Then I pulled my arm out quickly and let the lid slam shut. I must've been kicking up the dust as I danced, because after the ritual was over, I had a bit of an asthma attack. I remember sitting on the floor and listening to myself as I wheezed.

Thirty years later, as I inched along the freeway through LA, the memory of that unsettled vow made my palms even sweatier. I loosened my grip on the steering wheel. As usual, the traffic was stop-start, offering me the chance to marvel at the visual familiarity of each exit as I drove past—every curve of the freeway, every building that rose up beside it, every sign and billboard. Like a painting that had hung at my bedside all my life, the landscape of LA was now etched firmly in my brain.

I'd lived there almost eighteen years and was intimate with the city's ugly, strange appeal. I knew once you step inside the muted grey box, there are sprawling pockets of vibrant green . . . powdered white art-deco structures with deep-red leather edges . . . messy neon pink-and-blue signs pointing to a vast array of cultures . . . sections of expensive, pristine order . . . and cutting-edge trends built into merchandise, fashion, and food you never knew you wanted or needed—until you realized such extravagance actually existed.

LA was my home, but not by choice; it was home out of necessity. This was the city that made the most sense, the city where most of the work could be found.

When I'd first moved to Southern California, I wondered where all the clouds were. The daytime sky looked like a flat mass of pale bluish-grey that grew slightly darker as night fell. Then, in the midst of the city, I could barely see any stars. I panicked a little. How could I live under such a lifeless sky?

Thank goodness, after some days, a few small, insipid blurs of white began to appear. The hope that some clouds could roll in made me feel like I was still on Planet Earth. That was a relief, even though my feelings of relief had no bearing on my actions—because leaving was out of the question.

Or so I thought.

❀

When I finally arrived at Joannie's office, she greeted me with an honest smile, a little squeal, and a hug. We sat down in her waiting area, between a small fountain in the corner and a coffee table that held one of those miniature sandboxes with a tiny rake. As always, Joannie gave me her time, her full attention, and her open self. She wasn't the kind of manager who liked to sit behind a big, frosty desk piled high with actors' headshots and contracts. Usually, in our office meetings, we snuggled up on her couch.

As we sat there together, I wondered how her face had remained so happy and fresh after all of her years in this ruthless business. Hollywood had depleted my supply of good feelings, much like it depleted other actresses' supply of fat cells, but Joannie was resilient, still plump with hope and promise. She even had a sweet smattering of dark brown freckles across her nose and cheeks. Her attitude was infectious, which was part of the reason I enjoyed being beside her.

We were friends, though not quite buddies. I was never fully relaxed around Joannie, but when I was with her, I didn't want to leave her—partly because I liked her so much and partly because I imagined she held the magic key to my success. I always had the feeling she might pull out that key at any minute, hand it to me, and tell me to unlock my fate. Perhaps it would

4

be a fate better than mere fame, more like the miracle that over-took Julia Roberts's career. I'd be known as the "it girl" of my time—an Academy Award winner who was also box office gold. I'd be a phenomenon: the new, bigger, better Julia Roberts. If I were to leave Joannie, I might miss that moment.

"So you're really serious?" she asked. "You're done?"

"I am," I answered.

I'd had what you'd call "nice success" on television. I'd been a series regular on a few TV shows—shows not many people watched, like *The Invisible Man* on the Sci-Fi Network and *Muscle* in the early years of The WB. I had a recurring role—multiple appearances—on shows some people watched, like Aaron Spelling's *Savannah* and *Seventh Heaven*, and I'd guest-starred on a ton of shows everybody knew, like *Seinfeld* and *Ned and Stacy*. I'd played juicy roles in television movies and miniseries. I'd voiced scores of animated characters, and in professional theater I'd been lucky enough to play some classic leading ladies, including Hilde in Ibsen's *The Master Builder*, Julie in Strindberg's *Miss Julie*, and Nina in Chekhov's *The Seagull*.

But ever since I'd delivered our first baby, Rafa, my desire to act had flown suddenly upward—not quite away, but hovering somewhere above me, in limbo. I continued to work on TV for two years, and I got the work done, but the shine around acting no longer shimmered as it once had. Rather than falling out of love, my lost desire felt more like impo-tence, like my dream was flaccid. Yet I was still terrified to fail.

Having to drop everything to audition at a time that was inconvenient for me, and having no control over my schedule, was the result of still being an actor for hire. I hadn't achieved the level of success I needed in order to call the shots, and that made my situation worse, my failure scream louder than ever.

I didn't want to lose my drive, but I couldn't bear to reschedule plans I'd made with Rafa, hire a sitter, and then prepare for and race to a last-minute audition. Sitting around sawdust-filled sets or uncomfortable outdoor locations while I waited for the last shot to be completed became miserable, especially knowing I'd missed Rafa's wakeup that morning and would most likely miss his bedtime, too. So, more often than not, I'd cancel the audition—and then be consumed with guilt over neglecting my career.

When my second son, Marco, was born three years later, I let the desire to act fly away, and up it went, too far out of reach.

"I might go back and get my nursing degree someday," I told Joannie on the couch, almost meaning it. "I wouldn't mind being a labor and delivery nurse."

Joannie nodded. Her assistants were answering phones in the other offices, calling out that so-and-so (an actor whose name everyone knew) needed to talk. Joannie had done really well over the years and had developed some A-list talent. That afternoon, I could sense a little restlessness on her part, but she told her assistants she'd get back to the calls and remained with me.

She was a good person. I'd worked steadily, and our actor-manager relationship had been mutually beneficial since the day I'd graduated theater school fourteen years earlier. Joannie once told me that while watching the Academy Awards, she'd confided to her husband that she believed only a handful of her clients had the chops to win an Oscar . . . and that I was in this prestigious group.

SHANNON KENNY WILL BE A

FAMOUS ACTRESS

"Nestor's a little nervous," I said, "because I'm taking my hat out of the ring."

"Oh, I'm not worried about Nestor," Joannie replied. She was getting twitchy now. "He's such a great guy, Shannon. He's so good, and he's doing so well." She paused, and I could tell she was wrapping up, just about to shift to the end of our conversation.

I wasn't ready.

"I know. I know," I replied, beaming broadly. "I don't know how I got so lucky!"

Meeting Nestor is truly the best thing that has ever happened to me. We have a great love, and I often marvel that I actually managed to find my partner during the chaos of building an acting career. Nestor is good and kind, and we make each other laugh—he is my favorite grown-up in the world.

His acting career was on solid ground. He was working steadily and continually gaining momentum, mostly on TV—and just a few months later, he'd land a role on the hit TV show *LOST*. He'd even nabbed some small roles in big movies, which was something I'd never been able to do. At this point we were putting all our eggs in Nestor's basket—the most successful basket, the basket we deemed most likely to succeed. The basket where it made sense to put the eggs.

One of Joannie's assistants came in quietly and handed her a message. She was a nice girl, but I could've punched her in the face.

I should've booked a lunch, I thought, wondering if I should just get up and leave. But I was frozen. *The new, bigger, better Julia Roberts* . . . The couch may as well have been quicksand.

The assistant lingered. Joannie read the note while simultaneously explaining our history together. "Shannon met Nestor on their first day of shooting a sitcom called *Muscle*," she said. "It was written by the guys who created *Soap* and had a thirteen-episode order, which launched The WB network." She turned back to me. "It was so sweet when you two met!" Then she turned toward her assistant again. "Tell them I'll call back in a second."

Joannie just did two things at once, I thought as the assistant scurried off. *Why can't I do that?*

And then my inner need for validation turned outward. Looking up at some movie posters on the wall, I saw another actress my manager represented.

"Wow. How did she just take off like that?" I asked before I could stop myself. "Now *she* has a career I wouldn't worry about."

The moment those last words left my mouth, my chest twisted up. Joannie didn't like to talk to clients about other clients' careers, which is a good practice. I was poking around at the edges of another actress's life, one that was definitely not mine.

"She's doing great, but all of our paths are different," Joannie declared. "You're a mother now."

My chest and my heart were actually starting to burn.

What's wrong with me? I thought. *Why can't I play it cool?*

And then it came out—the real reason I had sat there long past my welcome, the real reason I had come.

"You're not even gonna try to talk me into staying?" I cried, my heart, my chest, my rib cage all on fire.

Joannie's face darkened a little, in a way I'd never seen before. I'd never given her any trouble in the past. Ever. I'd always been a good soldier. I was going to be one of her Academy Award winners! At the very least, I'd become her journeyman actress. And now I was sounding like some kind of deranged, bipolar, needy ex-lover. Wasting her time. Sending her weird mixed signals. Begging her to beg me.

"This is your decision, Shannon," she replied firmly. "It has nothing to do with what I want." She paused, sitting there in confusion.

The truth is, I'd been lying to Joannie all those years. Sure, she'd seen me genuinely disappointed—devastated, even—in the moments when I'd lost out on a job. But I'd always presented myself as a person who had her head and heart under control. I'd rarely let her in on my grief. She had no idea of the high stakes I'd set up for myself at the age of twelve—stakes I had never let go of, even now.

SHANNON KENNY WILL BE A

FAMOUS ACTRESS

Joannie opened her mouth to continue, but I cut her off with a shrug and a laugh as I squeezed her arm and wrenched my butt free of the couch. Things had become awful and awkward. I needed to get out of there.

"It's okay. It's okay. I'm fine," I reassured Joannie with perky resolution. "I'm making a nonregrettable decision."

But inside I was crying out, *It's over. It's over. It didn't happen. After all these years—after writing down those words, my sacred vow—it didn't happen. And now it's over.*

I hugged Joannie hard, with a giant smile frozen in place. My heart still twisted painfully, creating sharp edges that tore a hole in my chest. Turning my back on her, I tottered down the stairs and out of the office in high heels I would rarely put on again. The ache had started, but it wasn't in my feet and it didn't come from my frozen smile. Instead it emanated from the hole inside me, made by letting go of my dream.

And I had no idea then just how big and painful that hole would become or how lost it would make me feel.

Chapter Two

JULY 2009

Three years after leaving my manager's office—and my career—our choice about which basket to put our eggs in was looking like a smart one. The boys and I were in San Diego, standing beside Nestor in a green room adjacent to a giant theater. It was Comic-Con, the largest annual comic and pop culture festival in the world. At the San Diego Convention Center, a venue big enough to house the 130,000 people who attend each day, we could hear the buzz of a massive crowd waiting in the theater next door. Some of the producers and cast members from *LOST* were there to speak about their various roles on the show, and thousands of people had shown up to hear them.

After Nestor had started as a one-episode guest star in season three, his character had been written into additional episodes that year and even more in the following two seasons.

He commuted to Hawaii, where the show filmed, while I stayed home with the boys, who were now four and seven years old. Anytime he was working while Rafa and Marco were on a school vacation, we jumped at the chance to fly over for a visit. But for *LOST*'s final season, which would be starting in a few weeks, Nestor had been offered a series regular contract. That meant the whole family would be relocating to Hawaii for a year.

I was excited about the move. On my visits to the island of O'ahu, we had discovered a town we loved, where most of Nestor's castmates lived, and had rented a house there, directly on the beach. We'd also enrolled the boys in a school where many cast members sent their kids. I'd been enamored with O'ahu every time we'd traveled there. Even if living there turned out to be nothing like visiting, though, we took comfort in knowing we would only be there for a year.

There was another reason I felt invigorated by the move: I was a diehard, never-missed-an-episode, number-one-on-my-DVR-list *LOST* fan. I'd loved the show from the beginning, long before Nestor joined the cast. Working in the industry for twenty years hadn't spoiled my ability to suspend disbelief. I still found it easy to completely immerse myself in the world of a good TV show, movie, play, or book. When I first met the actors on *LOST*, I had to mentally prepare myself by running over the truth in my mind: *It's Jorge—not Hurley. It's Jorge. Jorge.* Or: *Don't call him Dessie—his name is* Ian, *you dummy! Remember that.*

The world of *LOST* was mostly set on a tropical island whose jungle was spotted with mystical relics, abandoned bunkers, shipwrecks, cages, temples, and hidden settlements populated by people belonging to strange subcultures. The characters—most of whom had arrived on the island via a horrific plane crash—were from different walks of life, and they were complicated people, written with heart. There were love stories, love triangles, and love squares. There were creepy cults, messed-up family dynamics, unexplained miracles, and time travelers. There were murders and wars, exotic animals and supernatural creatures, and more—and then even more. The writers had set up very wide perimeters for the *LOST* universe, and their imaginations seemed to run wild. But they always kept the characters' overriding motives simple and profoundly relatable.

The stories were packed with imagery and symbolism, references to reoccurring numerical patterns, biblical stories, scientific and philosophical theories, and mythologies. Yet it was the underlying theme that hooked me: the battle between good and evil, that pull in our own human nature between our light and our darker selves—our shadow, as described by Jung. Shakespeare often wrote his characters with this deep duality, and they were the best ones to play and to watch. So naturally, even before it meant watching my husband on the show, I was captivated by *LOST* and looked forward to it every week.

The show was not real life, of course—far from it. Still, as we prepared for the move to O'ahu, I thought about being there on the *LOST* island and enjoying a front-row seat for the making of the show. I started to fantasize about wriggling my seat forward a little so the chair's front legs straddled the line between my life and the *LOST* world.

It wasn't a fully developed fantasy—just a wish to escape what my day-to-day existence in LA had become. Which is not to say I hated my life. In fact, in so many ways, I was grateful for it: I enjoyed being with my friends who were also moms. I was relieved to escape both the pressure of constantly looking for the next gig and the rejection that often followed. Watching the boys grow was fulfilling; that unique parental love was absolutely like no other. I was satisfied with being their mom . . . almost.

My problem was with the silences—the moments when I was pulled up at a traffic light with both boys asleep in the back seat. It would be quiet, as though everything else had stopped, and my mind would be clear, but there was nothing to think about. Or I'd be in the shower, with my mommy checklist done, and I'd have time to reflect for a moment, but all that would arise were clouds of steam—and pain and emptiness from the hole in my chest.

And there were a lot of silences.

My silences used to be filled with ideas and thoughts that would fly in and out of my mind, of their own will. I'd be working on a character for a play, a TV show, or an audition, and I'd think about something my character would say or do. I'd imagine the reasons that informed her actions in the script, something in her day-to-day life or her past life, and I'd play them all out in my head, detail by detail. I'd imagine anything that had to do with the text that rounded out my person's life so as to better tell the story—the story I was being paid to help tell. And now I had no characters to work on, no stories to tell, and I was earning no money. My mind felt still and I was frightened. I was Nestor's wife and Rafa and Marco's mom, but I couldn't grab a hold of *me* anymore, of who I used to be in the stillness.

It seemed sophomoric to be forty and suffering a crisis of identity. And I felt ungrateful. Nestor and I would make less money without me working, but we could sustain ourselves, I'd be able to stay home with the boys, and we were almost positive we'd be able to continue to pay our mortgage. I was in a position of choice. And now I'd be spending a year living in paradise. How dare I make a peep?

Still, I began to see my life as insignificant. I was part of a very big group—just one of many millions of moms in the world. It was an easy gig to get. I wasn't separate from the rest. I wasn't special.

Even as I had these thoughts, my need to be elite repulsed me. One of my closest friends in Australia had suffered three miscarriages and was undergoing IVF. Motherhood for her was a difficult gig to nail down. I reminded myself of her condition continually, but it failed to fill me with gratitude. What a narcissistic asshole I was. Where was my compassion for my friend? And why was I still feeling the need to shine above others?

SHANNON KENNY WILL BE A

FAMOUS ACTRESS

Had that twelve-year-old girl brainwashed me with a need so ferocious and so enduring it invaded every cell of my body, becoming a part of my DNA? Like a spoiled child with permissive parents, I'd never stopped myself from seeking to fulfill that need. Would I ever be rid of it—and did I really want to be?

At the very least, I didn't want her to show up at Comic-Con.

We were there to support Nestor. But I couldn't shake the twelve-year-old me that day. She was front and center in my psyche—the unseen star of my own personal drama.

There was excitement in the air. I could feel it seeping from the Comic-Con audience, under the door cracks and into the green room as we waited for Nestor to take the stage. I was corralling the boys out of everyone's way when I saw a familiar face beside us: Jimmy Fallon.

I chuckled to myself, thinking, *What a coincidence.* Just a few days before, Nestor and I had been playing "Don't Fear the Reaper" by Blue Oyster Cult on our Wii *Rock Band* with the kids, which prompted us to show them the *Saturday Night Live* "Cowbell" sketch on YouTube. They thought Will Farrell was funny, gyrating around with his big bare belly and banging on his cowbell. And Nestor and I were especially drawn to Jimmy Fallon, who was hysterical, trying to deliver his straight-man lines without laughing.

He had a camera crew with him now, and his face looked camera ready with a layer of pancake foundation. I figured he was there to get a quick interview with the cast, who were huddled around a convention staffer, being prepped for their panel. At the moment, though, Jimmy was standing there just doing nothing. I was standing there just doing nothing too, even though Marco was climbing up my leg and Rafa was using one of my arms as the stabilizing bar to his human bungee cord.

So I decided to say hello.

I introduced myself and the boys, telling Jimmy that we'd just shown them the cowbell skit and that they'd loved it.

"Oh, is that right?" Jimmy replied sweetly, nodding. His smile was so genuine.

Then one of the boys farted.

And it was ripe, and we all smelled it. And I knew it came from us, and Jimmy knew it didn't come from him. And all I could think was: *He probably thinks it was me.*

Suddenly, my desire to be perceived as a frighteningly talented, timeless beauty with a savvy intellect and limitless potential who, after having children, had no choice but to succumb to her truest mothering instincts and quit acting so she could be selflessly uber-present in her boys' lucky lives . . . had been foiled by a wall of fart. And an immediate need to get my kids out of there and walk off the stench.

Why was I acting like such a star fucker? I'd never glommed on to famous people in the past. I'd always wanted to *be* the star, and being friends with a famous person was not the way to achieve that goal.

Still, whenever I'd been with famous people at a dinner or a party, time had always felt suspended. Those moments in the presence of the truly famous felt like inhabiting a brightly lit prism, where everything else important in my life fell away. This happened even when I didn't respect the work of the star in question. And with Jimmy Fallon—who, incidentally, I thought was a brilliant comedian—I'd wanted that out-of-body experience again. I'd wanted out of my life, just for a moment.

But life had intruded in the form of a fart.

As I walked with the boys out of the convention center, reality rushed right back in. On the San Diego streets, I became one of the mother-pack again. Out there, tons of moms and kids swarmed all around. And I hated that place. I hated myself. And even though none of it made sense, I hated my kids and Nestor, too.

On the drive home from Comic-Con, as the kids were sleeping in the back seat, I vented to Nestor. "I don't know. I just feel like a whole lot of nothing," I complained. "Why couldn't I be a good multitasker like so many working moms?"

But I knew my discontent wasn't really about that. I was trying to say something else entirely. At that moment, on the heels of watching my husband being fawned over by thousands of fans, of sidling up to Jimmy Fallon only to face humiliation, I was really saying I wanted success just like Nestor's. I wanted success that was perceived by the outside world.

SHANNON KENNY WILL BE A

FAMOUS ACTRESS

I still needed that extra bit of self. I'd been trying to grow up and grow out of it, but I still wanted some of the attention. I wanted it badly.

Even as I complained, I simultaneously shamed myself for playing the fool—for having babies while not realizing *I* was still a baby. An idiot, really.

And soon we would be heading to Hawaii, and suddenly the silences seemed even more terrifying. It would be even quieter at the stoplights, with no billboards to read, no helicopters overhead, and no cop cars speeding by to distract me.

The islands were commanding—as though the land required you to quiet down and take notice of it. And taking notice would still my mind, and that would create more silence.

"I'm really scared about Hawaii," I confessed to Nestor.

"It's going to be great," he replied, "and it's only for a year."

"Yeah."

I had nothing else to say. I'd talked myself around and around my dissatisfaction so many times, and I knew this conversation ended right where it began. That was the nature of being lost.

Nestor was done talking. He'd spent the past two days on display, and his tank was empty—I could tell. Hawaii was happening, whether or not I was ready. I'd just have to be lost in the midst of *LOST*.

Then again, when their plane crashed on the *LOST* island, the show's survivors underwent enormous physical and mental changes, sometimes ending up entirely transformed. One character, John Locke, enters the plane a paraplegic and then, after it crashes, exits with the ability to walk again and with an entirely new take on life. Perhaps the physical shift would jolt my brain into a place of lucidity and certainty. I sighed. *If only . . .*

But the contracts had been negotiated, our lease was signed, the boys were enrolled in school, and the plane tickets were bought. Whatever the future held, there was no turning back.

Chapter Three

AUGUST 2009

August was our departure month, the month of our big shift. As we were leaving for Hawaii, I was faced with two choices: to put the past to bed and embrace the change, or to resist the change and ask the coroner to redo the autopsy on the corpse that was my career. I knew what the healthier choice was, but I was still wrestling with so many questions.

Namely, what was that twelve-year-old me thinking?

If I'd known what it actually took to become just a *working* actress, would I have even wanted to take a shot at becoming a Famous Actress—or even an actress at all?

I didn't know back then that to secure work as an actress, I'd need the following things: talent, training, nerves of steel, an unwavering desire to work, the right face, the right body, the right face and body "of the moment," and the right role at the right time. In other words, certain people in power would have to be enamored with my work and my personality, and those certain people in power would have to want to sleep with me.

This last criterion was not literal, of course. But the powerful people would have to find me "fuckable" in order for me (or someone of my type) to book jobs. The more sophisticated executives probably told themselves they were looking for a girl with that beguiling "it" factor—some enchanting, irresistible magnetism that drew their eyes to her—but what they really were looking for was fuckability.

Becoming a Famous Actress required all of that, plus a delicate alignment of creative choices with salesmanship that would persuade millions of people to pay their hard-earned dollars to see your movies or to turn on their TVs to watch your shows. And it all had to happen within a short, specific time frame, because almost nobody in Hollywood finds a woman fuckable at forty.

As daunting as this truth was, the knowledge wouldn't have stopped me from pursuing my dream. Nothing, in fact, would have stopped me.

I met Kerrie, one of my closest lifelong friends, on our first day in seventh grade, and with an unspoken promise to keep no secrets from each other, we quickly became kindred spirits. Kerrie never dreamed of a big life. She didn't suffer from delusions of grandeur. She had what were called "realistic aspirations," although today we'd probably say she had low self-esteem.

Kerrie was not an academic, school work was torture for her, and her plan was to leave school in tenth grade for secretarial college. This was not unusual in our Aussie beach town. About half of our tenth grade went directly to TAFE (Technical and Further Education) to pursue a career in the trades, such as construction, cooking, accounting, and auto mechanics.

One night, Kerrie and I were having a sleepover when she asked me point-blank about my desires for the future. "What are you going to do, Shannon, if you don't become a Famous Actress? Are you going to be okay?" She slurred the words "famous actress" a little, as though saying them sincerely for the first time. She had one of those clipped, singsong Aussie accents, but she spoke in a low, guttural tone, trying to give the words gravitas for my sake as we lay there in the dark.

I was silent for a while as I stared into the blackness. I'd never thought about the possibility of failure. "I don't know," I answered with equal gravitas. "I'm just going to have to do it."

The truth was, I had a pretty good run in my school years. I was an overachiever who had grown addicted to doing well. All through school, I loved the honor of being the last one called up to receive my math test because I had gotten the highest score. On the final night of my theater group's annual pantomime, I held my breath as our teacher announced the winner of the best actress award. I feigned shock and delight even though she called my name every year. I imagined that would be what it felt like to win my first Academy Award.

I'd always wanted to be singled out, to be special. It's not that I was ever in competition with anyone else. I had a group of kind girlfriends who are my best friends to this day. But up on that stage, I wanted to be seen through a different lens, perhaps with a wider aperture so I appeared sharply in focus while everything around me was a little blurry. Even for just a short time.

My girlfriends and I danced in the jazz ensemble too, where we were taught to perform our moves in precise synchronization and identical positions. I danced as we were meant to, but I also tried to affect a special inner glow, and I secretly peered out at the audience to see if all eyes were on me. Thank goodness I kept my ridiculousness hidden, because if my friends had known what was going on in my ding-dong head, I'm sure they'd have unfriended me in a minute.

I became obsessed with being special. I started ritualizing, playing mind games with myself to see whether the good luck would continue to go my way. One of these games had me spending a great deal of time sitting on the *bog*—Australian for "toilet" or short for *bogatorium*, as my dad likes to call it.

In the house where I grew up, the floor beneath our toilet was made up of hundreds of tiny square beige tiles. As I'd sit there, legs dangling (and when I got older, with my toes touching the ground), I'd count the tiles as they ran horizontally, from wall to wall. These tiles were as small as pennies, and the rows were crooked. I could never get an accurate count of the numbers in each line. So I'd play roulette with the tile count and put forth a question, the answer to which would be determined by the result: Odd numbers meant *I will*. Evens, *I won't*. The questions varied only slightly.

"Will I win best actress in the end-of-year play?"

"Will I be given a solo in the classical dance ensemble?"

Sometimes I even dared to ask, "Will I become a Famous Actress?" But if I lost the tile count on *that* question, I'd just count again until the number came out right.

I began to count a lot of tiles in a lot of different bathrooms. And throughout high school, I generally managed to come out on top. But I always carried the feeling with me that I was narrowly avoiding defeat, forever wiping my metaphorical brow—wondering when the other shoe would drop.

One day, when I was in ninth grade, a young male substitute teacher approached me at our school store. As I waited in the long line with my friend Jenny, he brushed up against me and stood there, shoulder to shoulder. "You know, everything is going your way right now, but it won't always be like this," he said. "As you get older, things are gonna change. And it's not always gonna be so great for you." Then he started to saunter off.

Huh?

I was perplexed. Why would he have said that? I had said maybe two words to him the whole day, yet he was suddenly as familiar as a lover in the way he'd stripped me down naked with his words. He knew my insides somehow, and he'd pulled them out of my skin and left them lying beside me for the whole school to see.

I looked at Jenny nervously.

"Oh, fuck off, you prick," she said under her breath, swiveling me around so my back faced him as he walked away. And we both let it go.

But after I quit acting, I found myself thinking a lot about that faceless teacher whose words still rang clear in my memory. I wondered if he would have finally felt vindicated that his prediction—*it's not always gonna be so great for you*—had come true. Would he have delighted in the hundreds of losses I'd suffered along the way? I hated that jackass for saying those words to me—a fifteen-year-old girl!—but odds were, almost three decades later he'd have no memory of saying it. So I hated myself more for remembering him. And I hated my lack of wisdom for wanting fame in the first place.

Why did I need so much to be seen? What was missing in me that made me yearn for that? Kerrie was happy. She laughed robustly all the time, and her greatest ambitions were to be a secretary and then to find love and have kids. And Jenny (one of the most loyal friends I'd known) didn't seem to care what anyone thought of her. Then, there was me.

Why had I, at such a young age, wanted eminence so badly that it had grown with me and become part of my makeup? I was a silly person—that much was obvious—who harbored a lot of anger and anxiety around my failure. And now I was heading off to supposedly support Nestor's job on *LOST*.

Why couldn't I be whole and simply stand beside my husband?

Ba-boom! The airplane wheels touched down with an enormous double thud, and we were on Hawaiian ground. As we stepped off the plane, I inhaled the familiar Hawaiian air, soft, light, and dewy—the softest air I've ever felt. It's soft in the "just right," Baby Bear's porridge kind of way—never dry but not too muggy either. The trade winds blow intensely or delicately (often depending on what side of the island you're on) and keep the average daytime temperature in the low eighties.

In the Honolulu airport, the concourses that take you to the baggage claim are called "breezeways." They are covered overhead, but the sides are open-air bridges with a short guard wall and wooden railings on each side. As I ambled along with the boys to begin our one-year stay on the island, that soft air hit me like the active memory of a good kiss.

Oh yes, I thought. *The air is really, really lovely here. Maybe this is all I need.*

Nestor was with us but so far ahead he'd become a small spot in the distance. Recently he'd been complaining about how slowly I'd been moving. I supposed he was right. But how could I move quickly when I was lost in a fog, in a maze? One step in the wrong direction, and I'd risk hitting a wall.

Nestor mostly moves forward with speedy precision, and I've rarely seen him lose his way. But when he walks through airports, there's something else entirely going on. When we travel by air, he becomes an extreme version of the craziest parts of himself. He suffers from acute paranoia about missing flights, even though he insists we arrive at least two and a half hours before domestic takeoffs—three and a half before international departures—and we've never, ever come close to missing a flight. He moves at supersonic speed but with very little clarity of thought. He takes a ton of wrong turns and makes impractical decisions, and we often end up lost. Despite all this, however, he insists on being in control. The boys and I have learned to just stand back and watch the mess unfold. At these times, we call him "Airport Daddy." It would be funny if it were someone else's husband.

We followed Nestor, at a safe distance, through the Honolulu airport, making some loops as he miscalculated where the baggage claim was—a baggage claim he'd stood at a million times. Eventually we happened upon it. Our bags rolled off the conveyor belt one by one, directly behind each other. So far, so good.

The actors union has a strict rule that a show's production team must send a car with a driver when an actor travels to a job. And as we exited through the airport doors, our car was right there waiting for us. To the boys' extreme joy, it was a white stretch limousine. They'd never ridden in one before, and their excitement was doubled when they saw the tiny colored disco lights embedded in the limo's black ceiling.

Our two LA cars were still en route from Long Beach, so we stopped at a rental place where Nestor picked up our temporary car. Then we caravanned to the house we'd leased, in Kailua Town, on the eastern or windward side of the island.

We traveled via the Likelike Highway, which cuts through the Ko'olau Range that rises up behind the capital city of Honolulu. The mountains run down the whole eastern side of the island, about thirty-seven miles or so. The drama of the Ko'olaus is that they don't mess around. There is no preamble. Rather, they ascend abruptly with razor-sharp vertical drops, and they are nothing but green. The peaks run along the sky like the jagged edge of a broken window, and when the sun begins to drop, they are silhouetted in the dusk like a Wacky Wire carnival game—where the player holds a loop in one hand and tries to guide it along the curves without setting off the alarm.

Whenever I drive up close to the Koʻolau mountains, their tips look so narrow and sharp I imagine snapping them off like a piece of peppermint bark. The mountain range is so extreme because it's technically *not* a mountain range, but rather the western half of an ancient volcano whose eastern half has long since slid into the Pacific Ocean. Looking up at the Koʻolaus with that knowledge, it all makes sense. Kailua Town is not on a mountain or below a mountain but rather *in* a mountain—inside the crater of half of an old volcano. It's as though the town were cradled in a giant clamshell, which is perhaps what makes it feel so enchanting.

We'd done the drive along the Likelike before, but on this day the mountains loomed much larger than usual, as though reminding us that the stakes were different this time, that this was no vacation. Our lives would be spent surrounded by the Koʻolaus, and they were telling us we'd best get used to them. We responded with awed silence.

Passing through the Wilson Tunnel and exiting on the other side of the mountains, we were hit with the incredible view of Kāneʻohe and our Kailua Town, down below and to our left. Beyond the two towns lay the shimmering, glittering blue, blue expanse of the Pacific. Dancing off the water were a billion tiny jewels of light. The ocean was putting on a show for us, giving us a little welcome jig.

The gravel crackled beneath the limo's tires as we followed Nestor into the driveway of our rental house. Kai Drive is an L-shaped street, and our house was in the middle of the short part of the L, the part closest to the ocean. The real estate agent's assistant, Faye, came to greet us and walk us through the house. She talked about its history, about the original owners who had raised six children there and had stayed long after the kids had grown up and left home. It was only when both of their health required full-time medical care that the owners had left, moving into a nursing home together. Faye said the family was always spoken of highly around town.

There are no hotels in Kailua, but home rentals are plentiful. We'd seen the house before we decided to rent it, back in March when Nestor was working in Hawaii. The producers had hinted to Nestor that his role might be needed for the whole final season, which would mean all of us relocating. March is generally an overcast month in Kailua, so the house and even the ocean had looked a bit drab, but something good radiated from it. The house had been left with a feeling, as if gracious people had given it life. There had been shouting in that house, laughing, bickering, talking, kisses goodnight. Kids had rounded its corners at high speeds and skidded down its hallways. The floors had been swept a million times, and the lamps had stayed on late while procrastinated homework was completed.

The house had not been updated since it was built in the 1970s, but it was well maintained and had been freshly painted. It had great bones. If it were a woman, she would've swum in the ocean every day to keep her heart healthy; her torso, legs, and arms would be strong and stretched and muscular. Her skin would be too brown, a little tough and lined from being in the sun and salt too often. But a facelift would be out of the question; she'd have thought it too vain, point-less. Everything was great as long as she could breathe and think clearly. That was the feeling of the house.

The wood-paneled walls, out-of-date appliances, and lino-leum surfaces still functioned perfectly well, even though they screamed late *Brady Bunch* episodes where everything was "groovy." The furniture felt comfortable, as though it had been worn down from the warmth of well-loved souls. The shelves were jammed with books; many of them were about the island and its birds or plant life, with sweet dedications on yellowing pages from friends who'd visited in years gone by.

The house was built in the Hawaiiana style of architecture, in a plantation-missionary blend: wide and single-storied with vaulted ceilings and exposed beams. All the living areas were open plan, and the house felt large and airy. The bedrooms and bathrooms ran down its southern side, except for one guest room and bathroom tucked away behind the kitchen on the north side of the house.

And then there was the view.

The view was miraculous. Sixty feet of windows ran along the back of the house, facing the ocean and stretching almost from floor to ceiling. As we followed Faye through the house, I could hear the constant crashing of waves, the rising and low-ering lilt of beachgoer conversation from the path alongside the kitchen, and the birds—so many birds, with unfamiliar and exotic voices. When we stepped outside again, I could smell sweet plumeria and dry sand. The house felt so alive, and I felt alive moving around it with the knowledge that we'd be there for a whole year.

Faye said goodbye, and I was left standing with the boys

on the back lawn overlooking the water. The grass felt spongy underneath my sneakers, and I just had to dance around on it. So I sprang up in the air into a little pirouette, then dropped back down into a deep plié with my arms open wide, only to pirouette again, hugging the air into my heart. I spun like this around the entire perimeter of the yard until the boys tried to tackle me and begged me to stop. But I was so happy I couldn't stop, and as I was spinning above the ground, I started to think.

Perhaps the jolt of leaving LA and coming to Kailua, to this house, to this ocean, was all I needed. Perhaps this was my real home, where I was meant to be all along. Perhaps now that I'd arrived, I could settle into myself, into who I was before I'd ever dreamed of acting—before I'd brainwashed myself into wanting fame. Could this simple shift in location offer me a quick cure? Could this island help me be found, help me experience life in a new way, like John Locke?

I started to wonder if I might not be lost anymore.

☙

The crescent of beach on which our house sat is about three miles long. Kailua is famous for its bright turquoise water, but at times the ocean is a pale mint green or a deep cobalt blue, and sometimes it is a block-pattern mix of different hues. The breeze on the beach varies too, from so blowy the swirling sand stings like little ant bites to perfectly mild and cooling, as though God had tipped some angels to steadily direct the wind with palm leaves and create the most temperate environment for beachgoers. On the rare day the trade winds drop completely, everything becomes eerily quiet. The water gets still. The air becomes thick. If the winds drop for more than a day, the air feels dense and heavy, like a swollen balloon that might burst at any time, unsettling the layer of moisture and salt that has collected on every surface like fairy dust.

On the day of our arrival, the water was a brilliant aqua blue, and it was choppy. That didn't deter us. The boys and I ran inside and convinced Nestor to take a swim with us. As we bounded into the ocean, I saw a small creature on the shore—it was a Portuguese man-of-war. In Australia, we call them blue bottles, and they are usually much bigger than the one I spied. Faye had told us, quite nonchalantly, that there might be a few out there.

"Their stings are not bad at all," she'd insisted. "It just feels like having a red chili pepper rubbed on your skin."

How would she know what that *feels like?* I had thought. *Why would she have rubbed chili pepper on her skin?*

Faye then cheerfully advised us that if we poured white vinegar on the sting, it would go away. But I remembered being stung in Australia. Blue bottle stings really hurt, and it took much more than white vinegar to dissipate the pain. Maybe the Hawaiian blue bottles have a bit more of the "Aloha spirit" and less of the bigger, deadlier vibe you get with the creatures from Australia. So I sidestepped the little blue bubble and its tail of goo and jumped into the ocean with my guys.

The water was rough, and as the boys attempted to swim beyond the shore break, the waves knocked them around. Rafa was struggling but staying afloat. Marco was not faring as well. Every so often his little head would disappear, and Nestor or I would pull him back up lest he be dumped hard on the sand.

We were all putting on a brave face, even the kids. I think we had the same instinct—that our enjoyment of this first swim was important somehow, that it played a part in setting the tone for the entire year ahead. Nestor and I were laughing too loudly and smiling too hard as we tried to keep our eyes on the kids while the waves pummeled us. It was all becoming quite stressful. And then, as the forced fun reached a fevered, hysterical high—it happened.

Rafa's scream of pain reached me just as he lifted his slender white arm now draped with dark blue tentacles.

I swam toward him, but he had already shaken off the man-of-war. Maybe they travel incognito in pairs, or just divide themselves like mutant killer cells so as to pack the biggest punch. Whatever the explanation, on my way over to Rafa, I too was stung. The creature attacked me from behind, slipping itself around my right upper thigh, and the pain was hotter than any chili pepper I'd ever encountered.

The sharp sting settled below the surface of my skin, and when it could find no exit, it seemed to dive deeper down, into my muscles and bones. At the thought of Rafa feeling what I was feeling, I panicked. How could his little seven-year-old body cope with the poison? I couldn't bear to think about it.

We raced into the house, and Nestor looked in the kitchen for some vinegar while I ran hot water over Rafa's arm and my leg. After some time Rafa's pain subsided completely, and he was left with some long red welts around his arm. He calmed down and even seemed proud of his battle scars. Meanwhile, my whole body hurt.

Finding sleep was difficult that night. Some of the toxins must have seeped into the glands in my groin, making me ache like I had a virus. The slimebag substitute teacher entered my mind once again. I imagined him sneering at the knowledge that I'd thought my struggle might be over just because the house and the beach and the ocean had set my heart aflutter. I saw him doubling over in hysterical laughter because I'd been stung badly in that very same water I thought might wash my pain away. Would he say that it served me right—that the poison in my body was reminding me I was still delusional to think I was special and things would magically bend my way?

Maybe we hadn't made the right decision by relocating here. Nestor had commuted in the past—he could've done it again. This was a big change. Big changes could cause big trouble, and I was already lost.

I tossed in our bed. The Advil wasn't working.

"Are you okay?" Nestor whispered to me in the dark.

"I'm in a little pain," I replied. "I can't sleep."

"Think of yourself as a baby in a crib," he said as he rubbed my back softly.

This is Nestor's trick for falling asleep. He imagines himself as an infant, back in his cradle, swaddled and sleepy. So I tried to imagine myself there. I saw the sides of my crib, and I listened to my breathing as it got deeper and slower. I lay like this, with my eyes closed, and felt myself drifting away . . .

All of a sudden, I zapped ahead in time. I was no longer a baby but a little girl alone in a tiny room, sitting on the toilet—my bare feet just touching the cold tile, my mind blazing with the question of whether something good or bad was going to happen.

I finally fell asleep by counting tiles.

Chapter Four

AUGUST 2009

When I opened the curtains in our bedroom the next morning, I was hit in the face—in the best way possible—with the Kailua ocean glistening in its signature jewel tone of turquoise. My eyes rested on the sea, hypnotized by the tiny flecks of light moving all around like a giant kaleidoscope. Then I remembered the man-of-war.

Raised welts wrapped around my upper thigh like red ropes, as though I'd been lassoed and stolen by some dark, perverted creature in the sea. At least I was no longer in pain. Running my fingers across my temporary scars, I thought about all the doubts I'd fallen asleep with the night before: doubts about whether we should've moved to Hawaii in the first place . . . doubts about my vow to be a Famous Actress . . . doubts about marrying, having children, and walking away from my dream. All these doubts rushed into my conscious mind, settled into their usual spot, and reminded me I might not be in Los Angeles anymore, might not be at the scene of the crime, but I was still lost.

I suddenly felt lonely. Where was everybody?

In the living room, the boys had already staked out their separate corners of the couch. They had found the TV remote and turned to the Cartoon Network. Though I hadn't been there, I knew exactly how this scenario had played out. Rafa, being the oldest, had made a dive for his preferred corner and possession of the remote control. Marco, who is more easy-going by default, had curled up on the side that remained. They would now stick to those particular corners for the rest of the year.

No matter how lost I felt, seeing the boys was always a mood lifter. I sat down between them. It was like a little shot of sero-tonin—the heat of their skin, the soft squish of their flesh, as I found their hands and wrapped their tiny fingers in mine.

"Look at that ocean, you guys. I'm so excited Nonna and Granda get to see all of this."

My parents would be flying in from Australia that day so we could all spend some weeks together before the boys started school. It was not the smartest time for their visit—we really needed a few days to settle in ourselves. I knew I should've scheduled things better, but I was excited for Mum and Dad to experience life on the beach in Hawaii with us.

"I've been missing them so much," I said, squeezing their fingers even tighter. "I hope you boys are this excited to see me after you grow up and have your own families."

"Oh, you'll be dead and gone by that time," Rafa replied.

Wow. I didn't even think they were really listening to me.

"Gosh, I hope not," I answered meekly as a small shiver shot down my spine, suddenly wondering if he had a special kind of sixth sense that let him see into the future. Rafa did have a strange all-knowingness about him . . .

"I don't miss you at all, Mama!" four-year-old Marco claimed cheerfully, not even grasping the concept of the future. And right then and there, the serotonin wore off.

"Where's Daddy?" I asked, slightly irritated.

The boys just shrugged.

I strolled around the house, calling for Nestor. First I looked in the little laundry room off the kitchen, in the spare room and bathroom beyond that. No Nestor. I knew he wasn't in our bedroom, so I walked back through the open living area toward another spare room at the south end of the house, all the while calling for him. I used my stage voice and I saw the kids jump. During my four years in drama school we took vocal classes three times a week, so I'd learned how to project my voice to the back row of a big theater. This voice is deep, loud, and resonant, and sometimes it scares them. I use it a lot for discipline. But for the life of me, Nestor never seems to hear when I call—or so he says.

He claims to be hearing impaired. He blames it on "cauli-flower ear" from an old wrestling injury, but I don't buy it. As I searched the house, I knew either he heard me and chose not to answer, or he had shut me out psychologically and had truly become deaf to my roars.

The worst part of it all was I understood why he was shutting me out.

Putting our eggs in Nestor's basket—he would work and I would raise the kids—was a joint decision. My instincts were to be with the boys; my heart was pulled in their direction. Nestor's career had been hurtling ahead of mine anyway. He was booking more high-quality jobs more often and making more money. It was a logical decision for both of us. The loss I felt *after* we made our choices was unexpected—that was the difficult part. And as Nestor continued to work, I began to resent him.

It seemed to me suddenly that I had lost a two-person race—a race I didn't even know I was in until I stumbled across the finish line and realized Nestor had already won. But Nestor had no idea he was in the race either. None of it was his fault, but as much as I tried to fight it, I resented him for getting to go to work, for carrying on with the life we'd both worked so hard to build when we met. I felt stuck, left behind at the kids' table while watching him dine with the adults. So I'd piled my frustrations on him, and on him alone. He sensed my resentment, and he'd been hiding out more and more. And I'd been getting angrier and angrier about it.

As I stomped into the spare room, I could feel the rage rising up my neck. I had an urge to break down the door, and the acceleration of my fury was startling even to me. I tried to slow down and contain my anger—anger that was unwarranted, anger that seemed to haul me along behind it at an alarming speed.

I shoved open the door. "NESTOR!" I boomed.

But he wasn't there.

"Oh my God, where is he?" I asked the air. "How does he just disappear like this?"

My anger led me out of the house and into the garage.

But deep down inside myself, at the base of me, at my core, I wasn't angry—I was scared.

I understood why Nestor was hiding. He was moving away from me because I was unable to control my resentment. I was wrapping myself in it, wearing it like clothes I hadn't changed in days, and the sour stench was stuck to me while repelling everything else.

❀

Back when Nestor was commuting to Hawaii, we had tried to stick to a "no more than two weeks apart" rule. But things didn't always work out that way. The cast of *LOST* was huge, and the locations were primarily outdoors, so weather and the actors' different demands made for an ever-changing shooting schedule. There were times when four weeks would go by, and because of reasons neither the show nor Nestor could control, he wouldn't be able to fly home for a visit. On one of those occasions, we were heading into five whole weeks apart, so I pulled the boys out of school and we made the trip to Hawaii for a visit.

At the time, I was done. I needed a break, and I missed Nestor badly. When we saw him at the baggage claim, he was beaming. But while baby Marco gave his father a huge smile and five-year-old Rafa jumped into his arms, I froze.

Even then, I knew better than to give weight to my resentments. I tried to fight them as we stood there facing each other, to thaw myself out. *Nestor is just working to feed our family*, I reminded myself. *It's not his fault the schedule keeps changing.* He'd even booked us a nice hotel. But I'd become too icy. I loved and missed this good, decent man—this man who I could talk to for hours, who made me laugh like no other—and yet I couldn't give him the warm greeting he deserved. I was stiff and irritable, and my mood had turned dark.

Just as I started to complain about my miserable flight with Marco, who had flown as a lap baby and had squirmed all over me for five hours, I spotted a familiar face at baggage claim. My inner *LOST* fan burst out from under the freeze.

Actor William Mapother played Ethan with just the right amount of creepy—*and* he happens to be Tom Cruise's first cousin, which gives him an extra measure of cool. But after a delightful chat with him, where I genuinely felt as sunny as could be, I went back to being stoic.

I was bummed Nestor had been a witness to my uncensored joy, and I was determined to cover up any future excitement. As we rode in the cab to our hotel, I just stared out the window like a spoiled mobster's *gumar*, pouty and bored—even as I secretly reveled in the brilliant city skyline of Waikiki as it twinkled against the blue-black night.

A few days later, Nestor's schedule changed, and he was called in to work unexpectedly. Although we were both disappointed, I decided to take the boys down to the beach. It was around Marco's naptime, and I could see he was sleepy, so I swaddled him and laid him on a lounge chair under the shade of a huge banyan tree. Banyan trees are all over Hawaii; their branches grow latterly and send roots down to the ground that look like Tarzan vines. They also have big, thick roots that tangle around and up along the trunk, which are great for climbing. If it's a mature banyan tree, like this one, it will hold a wide, glossy green canopy that offers perfect shade.

We were at a small cove near Diamond Head, and the water was calm, just lapping lightly on the sand. At the edge of the beach, a little man-made sea wall had been built from big, rounded volcanic rocks. Many tiny, flat rocks peppered the shore. It was prime water for skipping stones, and Rafa was eager to learn.

We took turns skipping our stones and then sat at the shore with the water up to our waists. We did this for two blissful hours, the whole of Marco's nap. The sun cast a bright yellow-orange light over the beach like an old Polaroid, and the air was warm and the seaside noise was fuzzy around us except for the clear ring of Rafa's little voice and the ripple of the waves. It was peaceful. And it was perfect.

I couldn't wait to tell Nestor.

But when he returned home that night, invigorated from his time on the set, I froze again. Just seeing him like that hardened me.

When it's all working well, an incredible camaraderie takes place on a film set. The crew, the actors, the writers, the director—everyone works in sync to tell the same story. Being a cog in a wheel that was turning nicely always gave me a high. To "put on a play" is a very youthful endeavor, and the people who do it with sincerity and truth seem to shine from the inside. Over the years I'd felt a great sense of belonging while sitting in a rehearsal room, in the wings, in the green room, or behind the camera with the cast and crew. Those were wonderful days of intense playfulness and laughter; there was a special whimsy surrounding those people that always made me smile. I missed that group effort. I missed contributing. I missed belonging.

So far, I'd found that being a stay-at-home mother was fulfilling but not gratifying in the way my work had been. My goal as a mom is to raise two men who are good and who will (I hope) go out into the world and do good things. I am working for our kids, for *their* story, for *their* journey, for the production of *their* lives. But it will be years before I see that come to fruition.

Acting is a childish career, one that doesn't force you to delay gratification or work for the long-term benefit of others. During those moments between "action" and "cut," I was a little doll in a make-believe playhouse, investing only in my character's journey. And on those precious occasions when a real spark would ignite between the actors, we would be able to ride the wave of electricity all the way through the end of the scene. The walls would disappear, and we'd step out of reality and into the world of the story. That was the moment you knew that you might have electrified the audience, that they may have gone along with you into the writer's made-up world, and that you'd serviced the script as fully as you could.

When Nestor came home from work that night, I could smell the spark on him. I missed the adult playground. I knew he had ridden the magic wave, and I felt shut out and angry.

A day later, after my emotions settled and I began to see reason, I told Nestor about those perfect hours Rafa and I had spent together by the water while Marco slept. I explained why I'd shut down the day before and the reason for my resentments.

Nestor understood, of course, and argued that fulfillment was way more important than gratification. It occurred to me, not for the first time, that my husband is a wise man. He understood I was having growing pains. He was patient with me, but we both knew my words would take me only so far. I needed to change my behavior.

My anger was childish, and every time I pushed Nestor away, he took a micro step away from me as well. Little by little, we were withdrawing from each other. He'd begun to hide his work life from me, and his work was a big part of him. If I continued on this path, I might push him away for good.

After that visit to Hawaii, I flew back to LA filled with resolve and determination. I would control my resentments. I would pull it all together and support Nestor in his work. We would be fine. But then I got home, and my mind was overflowing with mom duties again, and I was busy and tired and frightened of my silences. The next time Nestor flew home, I walled him off again.

This pattern continued, until there I was a few years later, in our one-year rental on Kailua Beach, calling to him in vain— and suddenly as furious as I'd ever been.

What are you doing, Shannon? What on earth are you doing?

With Nestor nowhere to be found inside the house, I marched through the front door and yanked open the separate outside door to the garage.

Relax, I told myself. *Pull back. Chill out!*

But I didn't.

Stepping into a storage room filled with old bikes, giant canoes, and dusty framed photos of someone else's life, I could hear the muffled sounds of a man shouting. I circled around the junk and opened yet another door at the back corner of that room. There was Nestor in a whole different storage room, rehearsing his lines.

"I've been calling to you forever," I said.

"I came in here so I wouldn't wake you up," he replied calmly. "I have a lot of yelling to do in these scenes."

"What about the kids? You'd never have heard them if they needed you."

"They knew where *you* were," he said simply.

Of course they did, I thought, *because I'm never allowed to escape like that.*

My insides were twisting up. Once again, I was starting an argument that was not really justified. It wasn't really Nestor's fault. But I couldn't dam the flood of angry thoughts.

You can come and go, but I'm always stuck here. Stuck here because of the arrangement we made—the arrangement that has you on LOST while I'm just . . . lost.

"Well, I can't believe you're working now," I said. "We have to pick up my parents today."

"That's why I'm working now." Nestor was trying to remain calm. "So I have the work done when they get here."

"You're overworking the material," I insisted.

His anger started to rise. He knew where I was going with this. "You worked just as hard when you were on a show."

He was right. I used to run my lines a lot when I was on a show. I loved going through those lovely wormholes in my imagination and playing there for a little while. I'd make exciting discoveries about my character, sinking deeper and deeper into her and out of myself. It was a gift to be able to travel around my mind this way. So many ideas would come to me about my character. These ideas filled my silences and allowed me to throw more weight over onto my character's psychic pile, making my own psychic pile feel lighter and healthier somehow. This process would wake her up little by little until finally I had fully breathed life into her.

Now my silences were just silences. I'd plugged up those wormholes in my brain. My life, once so big with possibility, now felt so small, and the burden of my smallness felt so incredibly heavy I was afraid my ego might just buckle at any moment under the weightlessness of it all.

"Well, I was worried about where you were," I said finally. "And we can't be late for my parents." Having made my pronouncement, I stormed out of there.

"All right, all right," Nestor murmured behind me.

On our way to the airport, I suggested he turn left out of our street. The day before, he'd turned right and we'd gotten lost. But Nestor turned right again, and again we lost our way and had to do a big loop to get back on course.

Don't do it, I told myself. *Let it go. Let it go.* But I couldn't let it go.

"Why can't you just listen to me?" I demanded. "Don't you trust me? Do you think I'm stupid? Are you threatened by my superior sense of direction?"

And to myself, yet again, I said, *What are you even saying?* But I still went on.

"Are you just being stubborn even though you know I'm right, or is your memory truly that bad?"

And then he blew. "Oh my GOD! *Stop!*"

"No, you stop!" I replied, which made no sense at all, as he'd really said nothing up until that point.

And then Rafa piped in. "Come on, guys. Get over it."

I turned on Rafa, who'd been a little moody in the past few weeks. I knew he was most likely anxious about the move, but I still said it: "Hey, you haven't exactly been the easiest kid to live with lately."

Marco giggled, and then I yelled at him for . . . I don't even know what.

Then I burst into tears. "I've been so looking forward to seeing Mum and Dad, and now you guys are ruining it," I sniffled. "You need to say you're sorry."

"So do you," said Nestor.

"Come on, guys," Rafa said again, wearily. "Just say sorry." We did.

I was way more out of line than Nestor, and yet I couldn't admit it. It occurred to me this visit from my parents might get very complicated. I knew once the plane arrived, and Mum and Dad stepped into the open-air baggage claim, we'd all stand there smiling, greeting them as if nothing were wrong. But things were not feeling as "vacationy" as I'd anticipated.

What felt like our unraveling might not be the greatest spectator sport.

Chapter Five

AUGUST 2009

As a young actress, when I'd just blown an audition at a studio or a casting office or a theater, I'd take solace in family. If I couldn't have work, at least I'd have love.

I was comforted by the thought of spending time with my family and by the fantasy of having a family of my own in the distant future—a man to love and perhaps even children to raise. Those thoughts lightened the devastating weight of rejection, which was simply a part of the job. Now, my fantasy was no longer in the distance, something to look forward to. It was here. It was now. It was my life . . . if I could just hold it all together.

Rafa's night terrors weren't helping.

In the weeks before we'd left Los Angeles, Rafa had been waking up in the night, screaming about bad dreams, probably caused by his anxiety over the move. It was only normal, and I hoped the problem would just go away once we arrived in Hawaii. Frankly, I'd forgotten all about it. But on the second morning of their visit, Mum and Dad revealed that Rafa's screams had awoken them—on both nights.

My heart sank a little. "Oh. He's still having night terrors."

Nestor and I hadn't heard a thing. Our bedroom was on the ocean side of the house, where the crashing of the waves overpowered all other sounds. A bathroom and a closet separated us from where Rafa slept. My parents, meanwhile, shared a wall with the boys' room.

"Pardon?" asked Mum, clearing her throat. I knew she was a little hard of hearing, but the "pardon" had become more of a habit. Invariably, she'd answer the question before the explanation was finished.

As she "pardoned," I felt my dad stiffen. Her habit was driving him crazy, but he was practicing patience.

"He's been having night terrors," I repeated a little louder. "Apparently they're a thing." I had asked the kids' pediatrician about it. If we woke him up to comfort him, he'd most likely fall back asleep into the same bad dream. "Dr. Warner recommended we just let him sleep unless he wakes *himself* up."

"It's a wonder Marco doesn't wake up," said Mum.

"I know," I replied.

"Well, that's beside the point," said Dad. "Moving is obviously causing him some stress."

"Yeah. Actually, Dr. Warner said the best thing to do is roughhouse with him before bed."

"Pardon?" Mum asked.

"ROUGHHOUSE WITH HIM." I started to mimic the

motions. "You know, wrestle and jump around and stuff. Release the tension."

Dad looked at me. Mum kind of sniffed. There was silence on their end.

Skeptical silence? I wondered. *Or concerned silence?*

My parents' reaction threw me off balance and filled me with doubt about my parenting skills. Was it normal to feel nauseated and nervous every time you found out your child's life was not free of pain? Did other mothers' minds go straight to helplessness like mine?

"Well," concluded Mum, carrying her tea over to the dining table, "he was screaming bloody murder."

Twenty-four hours later, Rafa started to scream bloody murder during the days, too. He became contrary and obstinate. If we wanted to go to the beach, he demanded to stay in. When we planned a day trip up to the North Shore, he insisted we go to "our" beach instead. When we didn't bend to his will—which was always—he threw a tantrum.

Rafa's behavior was completely out of character. He is an easygoing kid, laconic and peaceful. My parents were shocked; they'd never seen him out of sorts like that. Their concern only grew as all of my efforts to correct his behavior failed: I tried to talk him down calmly. I timed him out. I held him. I screamed with him in sympathy. I screamed *at* him in anger. I attempted to guilt-trip him by weeping in frustration. I did everything short of slipping him a Xanax—but nothing worked.

Then my parents started to offer up advice. I reverted to my sixteen-year-old self, shooting down their suggestions because I, of course, knew better. Their advice felt like judgment, because deep down inside I feared I was disappointing them with my performance as a mom. And somewhere among all that crap, I had genuine concern for my boy, who was flailing.

Then Marco started to act strangely too.

We'd send him off to brush his teeth before bedtime, and he'd disappear. When I went to look for him, I'd find him wandering around the house as though he couldn't figure out where the bathroom was. The house in Hawaii was bigger than our home in LA, but could he really be losing his way around?

Worse than that, Marco was developing a fear of loud noises. A lot of wind whipped through the house—every bottom window was made with wooden or glass louvers so the ocean breeze acted as natural air-conditioning. Sometimes the wind was fierce, and doors would slam shut with a sudden bang. Every time this happened, Marco dropped to the floor as though he were a soldier who'd just returned from 'Nam. We'd have to scoop him up off the ground like a little rolled-up caterpillar and calm him until his heart stopped racing.

Amid all this, Nestor was stealing away as much as he could, claiming he had "homework" to do. I was pissed off at him for bailing out—my resentments were in full swing—but I could only get so angry lest my parents pick up on the energy and realize my marriage was becoming strained. I was pretending to them that my full-time mom status wasn't a struggle, that I didn't have a big hole in my chest. Pretending I was on solid ground.

Meanwhile, of course, I was lost.

Everything felt so fucked up.

Then my dad started doing something strange. He'd mention other Australian actresses who'd recently made news by landing big roles in American films and TV. Not the huge names like Nicole Kidman and Cate Blanchett, but lesser-known actresses like Melissa George and Isla Fisher. Dad reads the paper every day, so he was well informed, but it was strange he was talking about that stuff. And every time he did, a knife stabbed at my heart.

Why isn't it me he's reading about? I thought. *Where did I go wrong?*

And I was back in the coroner's basement, asking questions at my career postmortem.

Maybe I shouldn't have left Australia.

What if I had chosen Juilliard instead of CalArts?

And on and on.

Dad certainly wasn't relaying the news to hurt me; he had no clue about my ambivalence toward leaving acting. I'd always told my parents I was fully squared away with my decision to quit. As far as they knew, becoming a full-time mom had left me with no regrets. But Dad's comments also left me wondering.

Is he attempting to connect with me by chatting about the business?

Or is he, like me, thinking about what could have been?

I'd always been his brave girl out there in battle, on a quest, in search of her dreams. In eighth grade, when it was time to pick elective classes and a lot of my friends' parents were encouraging them to take home economics and sewing, my dad steered me toward commerce and French. He'd always persuaded me to jump big and far out into the world. Was he sad because I'd lost my fight, laid down my sword and retreated? Had my decision to step away from acting caused *him* to lose something too? The notion only compounded my pain.

The kids were having trouble settling in—it was to be expected—but with everything else piled on top of that, I hardly knew what to do with myself. I retreated to my room each night, grateful for the solitude, grateful for the time to spill my mixed-up insides onto the bed beside me so they could lie there for a while in chaos, to be dealt with at a later date.

One Friday night, the second week Mum and Dad were with us, Annie and Ian Cusick invited Nestor and me to a small pizza party at their house. Ian played Desmond Hume on *LOST*. Desmond was one of my favorite characters, and Ian played him flawlessly. His wife, Annie, was a friend of Nestor's and was expecting us, but she had no idea my parents were in town. On impulse, I suggested that while Nestor and I were at the Cusicks, my parents could go out to a restaurant for dinner alone. My suggestion felt wrong; I should've simply called and asked if Mum and Dad could join us. But I was anxious about imposing too many people on them—especially when I'd never met them before.

I waffled back and forth on the decision in front of Mum and Dad, which made them uncomfortable. I knew I should include them, but I didn't. They took the higher ground and pretended they were good with a dinner alone that night, even though I suspected I might have hurt their feelings.

When we arrived at the party, I discovered Annie was easy and kind, and her friends seemed the same. I immediately realized she was the sort of person who wouldn't have hesitated for a moment to have my parents join in. But it was too late.

We picked up Mum and Dad from the restaurant, and at home I stole away to my room as usual. Then I stopped myself. My parents had already headed out for their nightly walk on the beach. Mum had given up on asking me to join her, but I knew she loved to walk with me—so I ran down to the beach to find them.

The sky was not quite dark; there was just enough light to see forms and figures in black silhouette. A warm wind was blowing off the shore, swaying the inky palm trees that were scattered up on the bluff where all the homes sat. It all felt new to me, and I realized that since we'd arrived, I'd yet to really be out in the Hawaiian night. I walked down to the water, where the heat of the day was still trapped on the surface layer of wet sand. The night water was cooler as it crashed into white foam, and the combination of temperatures created the illusion of a little cloud of steam rising. The dark, moist air felt loose somehow, as though it were suddenly freed from the confines of the daytime sun.

Up ahead I saw two figures walking away from me: Mum and Dad. They were holding hands while listening to their respective iPods. I ran to catch up, giving them a wide berth before I called to them, so as not to frighten them.

"Hi, guys," I said, popping out in front of them.

Mum still jumped—she had always been skittish. "Good Lord! You scared me half to death," she said loudly with her earphones on.

"Shanny!" exclaimed my dad, removing his earphones. "Look how beautiful it is out here, mate!"

"Be careful you don't trip on anything," warned Mum. "It's really dark now. You missed all of the light."

"I know. I wasn't as tired as I thought," I lied.

Looking up into the darkness, I saw the sky had become a blanket of stars, so numerous and jammed in so tightly they seemed close enough to touch my nose. I was sure I could see the actual curve of the planet, as though each star had pierced the atmosphere with such precision and clarity, together they had dot-painted the earth.

"Oh my God!" I exclaimed. "Look at those stars."

"I've been looking at them for days, Bubby," my dad murmured. "Have you ever seen anything like that in your entire life?"

He *had* been looking up at the night sky a lot since he arrived. He'd been sitting out on the back *lānai*—a Hawaiian porch or veranda—drinking a beer and blasting the soundtrack to *Cinema Paradiso* on his portable speakers. Seeing and hearing him out there had been driving me a little crazy as I holed up in my bedroom and attempted to shut out the world.

Mum, too, had been driving me nuts, in a different way. She had gotten into the habit of breaking out into song—usually a song containing a word or phrase that matched the word or phrase she'd just heard in conversation. When I said I was going to run to the shower to wash my hair, she had burst out into a rendition of "I'm Gonna Wash That Man Right Outa My Hair" from *South Pacific*.

And it got worse from there. One day, we met our next-door neighbors, the Cartwrights, and learned they had relocated from Hilton Head Island only a few weeks earlier. Knowing little about the area, I asked whether they'd moved because it was too rustic. They explained that in fact Hilton

Head is quite hip—one of the most beautiful and desirable places to live in the whole country—and they'd moved simply because they thought Hawaii might be an even more wonderful place to live.

I looked at them in silence, awed by their courage in skipping from adventure to adventure.

Mum asked where Hilton Head was. When they answered, "South Carolina," she broke into her best rendition of Judy Garland's "Carolina in the Morning."

I quickly concluded it was time to go, wrapped up the conversation, and scooted little Judy inside.

Where did my mom find the confidence to just let it all hang out? I hadn't sung in front of strangers for years. In the past, when my parents had taken me to a musical, Mum and I would spend the next couple of weeks singing every song from the show together: at home in the kitchen, and even when we went out shopping, arms linked as we walked through the city. When had that ended?

That night, as I joined my parents on their beach walk, I couldn't have loved Mum more for continuously breaking out into song, or Dad for gazing at the stars all night. Out there on that dark beach, I saw my parents as brightly and clearly as I ever had. They were soaking in Hawaii with wide-open eyes—older eyes that I'd noticed were more lined and deeper set every time we reunited. Watching them age always shot a pang of regret through my body: regret I'd left our country behind, regret I didn't call enough, regret our conversations didn't linger longer. But that night, as the three of us walked on the beach, I marveled at them. And they were glorious.

❀

As I climbed into bed that night, I opened my nightstand and pulled out a gold leather-bound diary some girlfriends in LA had gifted me at a going-away dinner in my honor. I searched for a pen and wrote my first journal entry since arriving on the island. I wrote about my walk with Mum and Dad, and about our visit to Annie and Ian's. That got me thinking about Ian's character on *LOST*.

At the heart of Desmond's storyline is a longtime romance with a woman named Penny. One of my favorite episodes of the whole series, "The Constant," (played with intelligence and an unfettered chemistry by both Ian and Sonya Walger) centers on their relationship. Desmond travels through time, but as a consequence there are periods in his real-time life when he is susceptible to brain aneurysms. To prevent this from happening, Desmond must find a "constant"—a person who, upon contact, will plug him back into his reality and provide mental stability. Desmond's constant is his true love, Penny—short for Penelope.

In Greek mythology, Penelope is the wife of Odysseus, who was lost at sea. Likewise, she was his constant, waiting twenty years for him to return. On *LOST*, Desmond learns that his life will be saved by Penny and that she'll be there to answer his call. Love is all he needs to survive. As I wrote all of this down in my journal, I realized I had five constants with me, right there in my house—five people who truly loved me and whom I loved. All I needed to do was turn to them, be their anchor and let them be mine.

I wasn't about to be anybody's anchor hiding in my room every night.

How had I gotten so lucky in love? It was a mystery, and that realization brought an enormous amount of gratitude.

After I finished writing, I turned off the lights and opened the curtains. Then I lay on the bed and hung my head off to the side so I could see all those amazing stars. I looked at them and looked at them until their edges started to blur. At last, I put my head on the pillow, and just as my conscious mind was falling away, I pulled out my journal again. This time I wrote in the dark, on a new blank page, almost in my sleep:

Stargazing. Don't forget.

Something inside of me knew it was time to look outward. I was relieved to be out from under the darkness—but it didn't last long.

Chapter Six

AUGUST 2009

E ver since we'd arrived in Kailua, I'd been talking about blending up some margaritas. The house came with a huge, shiny blender that had a sharp industrial blade and a big black rubber lid that looked sturdy and reliable. It was a much better blender than the one we owned at home. All of my margarita talk finally led to a decision: It was time for Taco Night.

We had just spent an easy day at home: lying out on the beach, swimming in the ocean, napping, playing board games. My brother, Sean, and his girlfriend, Sally, had arrived in Hawaii to join the family and enjoy some vacation time before the boys started school. All of our leisure and rest time was making us hungrier by the minute, so the eight of us loaded into the minivan and set off to the market to purchase the necessary ingredients for a big dinner.

Mum and Sally cooked while I meticulously measured out the portions of tequila, ice, triple sec, and lime juice, looking up now and again to do a quick scan of the room, checking to see where the boys were. Like many moms, I tend to do these visual checks on automatic pilot, at least twenty to thirty times a day. But at some point, stepping away from the blender, I noticed that while Rafa was with Sean in front of the television, there was no Marco.

"Hey, Rafa, where's Marco?" I asked.

"I don't know," he answered.

"Nestor. Nestor!" I called.

He had disappeared . . . again.

"Nestor!" I yelled.

"Yes?" came a voice faintly, from the far right corner of our house. From our bedroom.

"Do you have Marco?"

"No," he replied.

I knew Dad was napping, but I went to his room and peeked in the door just to check. He was asleep on his bed. I met Nestor in the hall as he shuffled out of the bedroom in his socks. We stared at each other blankly.

"Nobody's with Marco," I blurted out. My mind went suddenly blank. I couldn't remember getting him into the car. Had he been in the van on the way home? My heart sank to the bottom of my stomach, and my breath started to quicken and shorten.

Oh my God.

It had been at least thirty minutes since we'd arrived home from the store. Marco would be searching the aisles for us, hysterical by now, thinking we'd abandoned him. Or he could've been abducted, and awful, awful things—things a child should never know about—might be happening to him at this very moment.

Oh my God. Oh my God.

I could feel my chest starting to heave. Did he come back with us from the market? I couldn't remember! There was so much going on. All of us had split up and headed down different aisles. Did I do my visual scan? We had a ratio of three adults to one child, for God's sake!

Had I been thinking about the stupid hole in my chest, about how useless and unsure I felt now that I was just a stay-at-home mom—now that I'd never become the kind of actress I'd dreamed of being? Did I sneak down an aisle to get away from the others and push my feelings down, so I could get a hold of myself before my family could see what was happening? I'd done that before, but I couldn't be sure about this time. What if, as a consequence, I'd taken my eye off my child—my four-year-old child—when no one else was watching him either?

"DID HE COME BACK WITH US?" I screamed.

"Yes," answered Nestor. "Yes. Calm down. I remember unbuckling him in the driveway."

Okay. Okay.

I tried to catch my breath. "What did you do next?"

"I don't—I don't know," Nestor fumbled. "I went into our room."

I wanted to scream at him again. *Of course you did! You went into that fucking corner like you always do! You work and you hide from me. You hide from me! You still get to work and create, and*

I don't, and you hide inside of it, away from me. And now look what's happened!

But none of those words came out of my mouth. Instead I just muttered, "Jesus," under my breath and ran to search for Marco. Nestor's mind had been on work, but our son was my responsibility, too—and my mind had been on margaritas.

❀

I'd felt the full weight of my responsibility as a mother since the morning of September 11, 2001. On that unimaginable day, I was heading into the second trimester of my first pregnancy. I woke up that morning with the same wish I'd had for the past eight weeks: that this day would mark the end of the morning, noon, and night sickness that had accompanied our firstborn's arrival in my belly. Instead, this day would mark something else entirely.

It was barely 6 a.m. when Nestor called me out of bed to watch the news on TV. Neither of us experienced anything close to the firsthand heartbreak felt by thousands of Americans whose loved ones found themselves inexplicably on the front lines that day. But like many of the minds and souls throughout America, something inside of us changed all the same. I felt sick in a whole different way. Suddenly, our safety could no longer be taken for granted. Being pregnant added extra weight to a grave situation.

Oh my God, what have we done? I thought. *How can we possibly bring a baby into all this?* I wanted to turn back time, to have had foresight about the terrorist attacks and stall getting pregnant for a bit. Everything was chaos, confusion, despair. As a country, we seemed to be scrambling.

America had always seemed to me like a stable family with wise and sturdy parents at the helm. In Australia, I had grown up watching *The Brady Bunch* and *Happy Days*. From the outside looking into that little TV box, America seemed like a bright and positive country—and heroic. In school, we learned about the propaganda that had spread after World War II, telling Australians that the Japanese (who had bombed parts of northern Australia and sent submarines into Sydney Harbour) would have invaded our country if President Harry Truman had not made the difficult, tragic decision to drop the atomic bomb on Hiroshima.

Later, in high school, we'd scared each other about nuclear proliferation, dared ourselves to watch the movie *The Day After*, and obsessed about Nostradamus's doomsday predictions. Then, in college, I looked on in awe as thousands of people gathered at the Berlin Wall, some tearing it down with their bare hands. At the student lounge, where news played on the large TV, I saw the speech President Ronald Reagan had given two years earlier—"Mr. Gorbachev, tear down this wall"—over and over as I grabbed coffee during rehearsal breaks. By winning the Cold War, America had saved us from turning into dust.

So I had long perceived the United States as a benevolent, charitable country . . . a protector against bullies . . . an ally to the good guy, to the little guy. America was Australia's friend and big sister. In America, anything was possible—that's why I had arrived at its doorstep to follow my dream.

But on 9/11, our wise and sturdy parents had fallen. Our

collective mom and dad were hurt, disoriented, unable to get up. For the first time since settling in the US, I didn't feel comfort emanating from the country, though I knew all its citizens were standing right there beside me. For the first time in my pregnancy, I carried the responsibility of being *the* parent, *the* leader. I was the one who needed to be strong, alert, and ever watchful. It was just Nestor and me and our little baby to come. We were that baby's lone protectors. This new feeling came with absolute dread.

After Rafa was born, I replaced dread with hypervigilance about his safety and well-being, though later that mellowed with experience until it was just vigilance, plain and simple. But a shift occurred in me, and I'm sure it happens with most new moms. A part of me—a part of my brain, my nervous system, my senses, my reflexes, my musculature, my skin, the hairs on my skin—a part of my whole self became devoted to keeping Rafa alive and well cared for. Even when I was at rest, this part of me, this percentage of me was on guard.

The feeling was disconcerting and uncomfortable at first, as though I had an itch that hid in the top layer of my flesh, right below the surface. I could feel the itch through my epidermis, but it was a little too deep to scratch. There was no way to relieve it. With time, my body grew used to the irritation, and the itch became a part of me. That's when I was ready to have another child. And the second time around, while I remained vigilant, I was a more confident mom, and I wanted to give my boys the very thing I had denied myself. I wanted them to have the freedom to let the other shoe drop, to fall down and have the courage to face it.

Even though I'd slip up as a parent at times—I'd get

distracted and the boys would fall down too hard or put something dangerous in their mouths, or I'd lose my cool and get crazy angry (which was sure to keep their future therapists' bank accounts full)—they were doing okay. And even through my ambivalence about full-time motherhood, and despite our recent setbacks since moving to Hawaii, they seemed relatively healthy.

But now, Marco was gone—truly lost.

By this time, I was sprinting through the house, screeching Marco's name but feeling strangled by each word. Sean and Sally were scurrying out in front of the house, where the kids sometimes rode their scooters or tried to catch lizards in the trees and on the fence. "Is he out there?" I tried to call to them despite my tightening throat.

My brother's voice came from a distance. "No."

As I searched every nook and cranny, a dark, unnerving bubble started to flow through my limbs and into my fingertips and toes, almost like adrenaline. But this was not the hot, electrifying adrenaline rush I'd felt in other situations—the kind that teetered between dire and exciting. Instead, this chemical was cold and hollow, as empty as the corners of the rooms where I'd hoped to find my son. It propelled me forward, but with little hope of escape. Darkness had descended and carried me over the threshold of a terrible place, and I needed to find the exit as quickly as possible.

Oh God. Oh no.

This can't be happening.

Where is he? Why isn't Marco answering?

No, no, no.

Fuck this stupid rut I'm in.

Fuck failed acting careers.

Fuck holes in my chest. Fuck depression. Fuck all of this ridiculousness.

Please just let me see him. Let me find him.

Where's my little boy? Where's my baby?

I staggered out the back door and was struck by the ocean's great expanse. The thought of Marco out there made me stumble. Of course, we would've been diligent about a pool, put a cover on it or fenced it in. But the open sea was right in front of us, and we'd yet to lock a door, put a gate across our path, or even talk to the boys about the dangers of those waters. How could I have dropped the ball so badly?

Motherhood was my job, my *one* job. This was it, the reason I'd left my career. There was so much work to do with the boys, but *this* was the foundation of my undertaking—the simplest, most basic thing I owed to these two little souls. I owed them life.

"Marco," I hollered, hearing my voice trail off into the wind. I ran down the concrete stairs of our narrow lānai and onto the coarse grass, tripping over my own toes. As I rounded the first corner of our messy, winding beach path, there he was.

Marco.

My heart thumped as loudly as I'd ever felt it, and all that breath that had been stuck tight in my chest fell out of me, carrying soft wails and parts of his name and mucus along with it. I knelt down and saw he was soaking wet, with a towel wrapped about three times around his tiny torso.

His thick-as-a-feather black eyelashes blinked. "Hi, Mama," he said. "I just went down for a little swim."

A little swim.

He was four.

A droplet of seawater fell onto his cheek, and his words rattled around in my head as I tried to make sense of them. Imagining his tiny body swimming out in the water alone, with his lonely towel on the shore—it was almost funny. I wanted to laugh, but I couldn't. Instead my hands gripped his arms tightly until my thumbs and fingertips were touching.

"Marco, you can never, ever, *ever* go down to the beach without Mommy or Daddy. Do you hear me?" I demanded. "The beach can be a very dangerous place, and you must *not* go near the water without us." I went on and on and on until I made him cry, explaining he could die out there and then there would be no Marco and everybody's lives would be ruined. Then I picked him up, cradled his little butt as his legs wrapped around my ribs, and felt his small, wet head nestle in the curve between my shoulder and my neck. I then carried him into the house.

At dinner, I tried to put it all out of my mind and just enjoy my family and Taco Night. But Nestor and I ate and drank very little and just looked at each other in dismay throughout the night.

Later, lying with Marco as he fell asleep, I flogged myself for loosening my grip too much. It was hard not to let go a little. I was starting to feel just the smallest poke of something brilliant and soothing coming up from the Hawaiian soil. But this was a reminder I had to stay on guard, just like I'd always done since I was young, because the other shoe could drop at any time. Pain could come so quickly, and with it the shame of failure and the loss of dreams. It was best not to get too carried away with anything, anything at all.

As Sean Penn once said while being interviewed by John Krakauer for the TV show *Iconoclasts*, sometimes the difference between being a good or bad parent is just luck. "You're a good parent if you encourage them to live life and be passionate and to be brave," he pointed out, "and you're a bad parent if the one time they do . . . they go off just wrong on their neck." The angle of Marco's fall had been in our favor that night. But holding him in my arms, I wasn't sure if I could put that much trust in the hands of fate.

At the obstetrician's office for a checkup in 2002, not long after I'd delivered Rafa, my doctor apologized for being late to my appointment. She'd had an extremely busy few weeks delivering 9/11 babies, she explained, exonerating herself. Many couples had clung to each other in those days after the attacks, perhaps not with my same feelings of dread but with hopes of creating new life. A small population boom had followed. Though America had been shaken and had fallen to its knees, many people had risen to their feet and quickly chosen life.

I was already pregnant in those months after 9/11. Otherwise, I don't think I could have made that choice, leaving it up to fate as to whether Nestor and I would make a baby. But I had immigrated to a brave country that had a lot of faith in itself. How wonderful the American people were!

As I lay with Marco and listened to both boys breathing in the dark, I felt soothed by the certainty that my whole family was asleep, under one roof, in a house on an island in paradise. I was an American citizen now. Surely I could do better. Surely

I, too, could rise and get up off my knees, climb out of my lost hole, and just move forward.

But that moment of certainty was ephemeral. Trying to move forward in those days had me crumbling at the slightest trip-up. The urge to remain sedentary—to freeze that one moment in time, listening to the boys sleep while the waves sloshed in and out, feeling Marco's rapid heartbeat in his small chest next to mine—was as hypnotic as watching the silhouette of the ceiling fan chase air around the room. The easy way out was to just lie there, to remain still and stuck. That seemed the only way to make such certainty last. I would've given anything to stay down, retreat from life, and make that moment last forever.

Chapter Seven

AUGUST 2009

My brother is a virtuoso in the sea. He swims with a flow that doesn't look human, especially in the ocean. Sitting on Kailua Beach with Mum, Dad, Sally, Nestor, and Marco, watching my brother dive in and out of the waves, it was hard to take our eyes off him.

Only Rafa was in the water with Sean, boogie boarding to his heart's content. I turned for a moment to Marco, who had captured a little crab and unknowingly squashed the life out of it with his clumsy four-year-old grip. Now he wanted me to wake it up. When I returned my gaze to the ocean, Rafa was riding a wave toward the shore, sitting perfectly upright with his board completely submerged.

Strange.

Rafa reached the shore, and then up popped my brother.

Rafa had been riding on Sean's back. His uncle had become his own personal dolphin. It was magic.

We all cracked up at the sight and agreed Rafa was a very lucky kid to have a shape-shifting uncle. But nobody was more spellbound than my dad. He was beaming, his eyes still fixed on the sea long after we'd all started up a conversation.

My parents had always been dream enablers. They watched and listened to my brother and me as kids and steered us toward our dreams. I'm sure they were not entirely mindful of their actions; they were only in their early twenties, unaware of child psychology in those times and far too busy to read a parenting book. They operated from pure instinct.

We didn't have a lot of money. My parents didn't put us into expensive specialty camps or hire world-class one-on-one tutors for us. But they saw what hobbies engaged us and the kinds of activities we developed an aptitude for. They took notice when we said we enjoyed something, and they found the best resources within our community for us to pursue what we loved. Looking back on it as a parent myself now, they were awe-inspiring.

As a child, I liked ballet and acting, so I took classes in our tiny suburban ballet school and neighborhood youth theater. My brother, who always loved the water, joined the local swim and surf clubs. My parents were proud of us and loved to have a little brag on our behalf, but they weren't stage parents—we were merely dropped off at our lessons and picked up later. Dad occasionally gave us the helpful lectures: *Stay positive.*

Think out of the box. Work hard. But that was it, in the beginning. For me, at least.

My brother was forced to perform under a little more pressure. Swimming and surfing are dominant Australian pastimes, and most Aussies live near the beaches. Sean's love of the water, his true talent for swimming, and our beach culture all united in perfect harmony so as to put the community spotlight on him.

My dad, who had grown up in the city as a talented rugby player, was aggressively competitive and projected that onto my brother. Yet while Sean was also competitive, I've always had the feeling he didn't swim just to be fast. He has water in his soul. He also has a tender heart that played against the brutality of competitive sports and the commercialization of athletes. I suspect his true nature may have been at odds with that part of the sport, and I believe the ocean—especially as he grew—became his greatest source of escape and comfort.

Hours of seeking the sea made my brother fishlike. I had once seen Michelle Kwan in a national skating competition, and her performance instantly reminded me of the way my brother swam. Other skaters were doing harder jumps and spins, but it looked as though they were fighting the ice, whereas Michelle was at one with it. For me, in a similar way, Meryl Streep's acting transcends craft and becomes art. She has an effortless ease that is different from most other performers in her profession. When I was young, I'd watch Sean glide easily in and out of the waves, transcending athletic ability. I couldn't name it then, but as I matured, I realized what we were witnessing: living art.

Dad reveled in our abilities, and there was something beautiful about that. One summer, between my third and fourth years of theater school, Mum and Dad came to see me do summer stock at Shakespeare Santa Cruz. Most theater companies do a few shows in rotation each summer, and it's typical for actors to have a large role in one play and a smaller role in another. My small role was to play a member of the court in the show *Amadeus*, but it was also my job to move stage furniture between scenes. The night my parents saw the show, I was sitting in the wings, waiting to enter and cross from downstage right, pick up a chair center stage, and exit with it upstage left. When I tried to stand up for the scene change, however, I couldn't straighten to a full standing position. The heel of my shoe had become caught in the hem of my long skirt.

There was no time to dislodge it—the changes were quick, and the chair had to be moved. So I hobbled across the stage hunched over, with my heel still stuck in my skirt, then picked up the chair and limped off. Later I found out that my dad, upon seeing this, turned to my mum and whispered, "Look at her. She's just brilliant, isn't she? Even while changing the set in the dark, she's developed an old lady character with a limp!"

As Sean and I had grown older, my dad had invested his heart in our dreams. I suppose if I'd been an artist, he would have framed every one of my paintings and declared them as good as Monet's or Van Gogh's. The support was encouraging, but with it came pressure and the fear of letting him down. Though his emotional investment in us was uplifting, there was always the risk we would fail and his hopes and dreams would be destroyed along with ours. With big love comes big pain.

The years went by, and our hobbies turned into our careers. While I was away acting, Sean had enjoyed great success as a professional ironman. However, high-endurance sports careers are short, and Sean had retired and was heading—or perhaps stumbling—into the second phase of his work life. Dad's way of helping us achieve success was to attempt to guide our professional choices, especially Sean's. He was trying to give Sean the advice and encouragement his own parents had failed to give him.

When Dad was in Catholic high school, a few of his Christian Brothers teachers recommended he attend a school for gifted students. My Nan and Pop didn't heed their advice, and my father ended up leaving school after tenth grade. But that didn't deter him. Being the most optimistic person I know, Dad put himself through three years of night school, eventually earning a diploma in Business Management. He was hired by Air India where corporate saw so much promise in Dad that they sent him to the University of Hawaii (of all places) to earn an advanced degree in Business Communications. My dad is a gifted salesman and recently, he'd been trying to steer my brother into sales-based opportunities with a sporting emphasis.

But Sean has the heart of an artist, and sales doesn't come naturally to him. He's no open book when it comes to feelings, but I could see he was acting like I did when Mum and Dad had attempted to give me advice regarding Rafa's meltdowns. We were adults now, and their advice made me frustrated and defensive, like I was sixteen years old and helpless.

That night after we'd watched Sean give Rafa a dolphin ride to the sand, the four of us sat on the couch talking after dinner: Mum, Dad, Sean, and me. Nestor had left for a few days of shooting night scenes on the North Shore; the cast members were staying up there and sleeping in a hotel during the day so as to avoid the long drive home after a night of no sleep. Sally was taking a shower, and the boys were asleep in their room. Dad and Sean were relaxing together, drinking a few beers. I could see the joy it gave my parents to have us both there with them, a foursome again.

It made me happy, too, but not relaxed. I sensed expectations in the air—an eagerness for this to be a bonding experience. The moments when it was just the four of us had become rare. It felt like Christmas Day or New Year's Eve—a bit *too* special.

As we sat there together, I started to feel slightly on edge, on guard. Dad had begun to give Sean some career advice. The four of us simply enjoying each other's company had turned into a family counseling session, and the head counselor had taken charge.

Dad had always been the clear head of our household. The problem was, the children were now adults—and there *was* no household. *That* was the reason, I suddenly realized, why the four of us sitting around the couch had felt slightly off. With Nestor and Sally gone, Dad had traveled back in time, and it felt dangerous.

Dad's advice about going into sales felt wrong to Sean, who didn't hesitate to disagree with him. It also seemed wrong to

Mum and me, so we backed Sean up. The debate carried on, and Dad began to get irritated—really irritated—as he argued his points. Nobody was backing down. I could feel a hum in the air. It felt as though we were riding slowly up to the crest of a roller coaster, but despite the huge drop ahead, nobody was putting on the brakes.

I looked down at the glass coffee table and noted that beside an empty beer bottle sat a glass of Maker's Mark and Coke, already halfway consumed. Dad had moved on to hard liquor; this was a bad sign.

Dad lectured on and on, and when we tried to refute him, he put his hand up and asked us to let him finish. When we finally spoke our disagreements, he stood up and began to pace. I looked at Sean and my mum, wondering if they'd noticed where this was heading. Was someone going to try to stop this?

As children, we were very respectful and obedient. We knew not to contradict my dad. Now that we were adults, however, I felt we were entitled to have our opinions heard. But I also knew there could be consequences. Dad was taking our rejection of his opinions personally that night, as though we were pushing him down. And when my dad is knocked down, he doesn't back off. He gets up and fights—not always fairly.

I was nervous now. The room seemed to be getting warmer. This could be bad.

We should back down, I thought. *Why don't we just back down?*

Dad's pacing then turned into circling. The rest of us sat there like three impalas trapped by a lion. We knew it was coming. Someone was going to get it. Yet even with that knowledge, we jumped at Dad's sudden change in volume.

"AH, BULLSHIT! WHAT THE FUCK?" he shouted. "Well, what do I know? I've only been in business for fifty years!" Then he mumbled something about being an "old fart" and made a faux exit down the hall—only to come right back again, ready for his next attack.

He lifted his finger and opened his mouth, ready to pounce. His castigation was headed straight for Sean, and it was going to be vicious.

I had to stop it.

"Not here, Dad. Not now. NOT in my house!"

I'd never really said anything like that before. Shutting him down and taking control of the household felt like a risky move.

It was met with silence. Dad just looked at me, sort of quivering. Then he spat, "What the Ffahh," and stormed into his bedroom, muttering something derogatory about me that I couldn't make out. The door slammed.

We all sat for a moment, just looking at each other like strangers. Seconds passed—could it be over so quickly? But then Dad was back out again.

"'*My*' house? '*My*' house?" he raged. Then he said something else I couldn't understand—something about how I wouldn't know anything about sales and about me sitting on sets—until he finally yelled out again. "Aahh. What have *you* ever done with your life?"

What . . . ?

Wow.

It took me a moment to absorb what he had said. I felt like my rib cage had been crushed. I knew it could get bad, but I had no idea it was going to get that bad.

What have you ever done with your life?

Here were the words that had been circling in my own mind. Here were the words I hadn't dared to ask myself, for fear of what the answer might be. And my father was throwing them at me like daggers.

"I've been in business fifty years," Dad continued. "Fuck you."

I drew in breath and stretched out the pause. And then I replied, "No, fuck you."

The voice that came out of me was deep, from the bottom of a place I'd never accessed before. We'd never said words like this to each other—ever. But it wasn't over.

"NO, FUCK YOU," Dad responded.

"NO, FUCK *YOU*," I said again.

And then he left.

And there was nothing.

I was so deep down inside myself that although Mum was crying, it sounded as though she were miles away. Even before the shock began to wear off, part of me marveled at how he was able to hit his target so precisely without knowing the turmoil I'd been going through the past few years.

The three of us sat there giving little comfort to one another; we were too wounded. Each of us eventually wandered off somewhere. I moved like a zombie toward my bedroom. I wanted to call Nestor so badly and ask him to come home, but the beach he was filming on each night had no cell reception. I cried and cried, trying to find comfort, but my body buckled over and onto itself, continually pulling me back into the pain.

I was struck by the coincidence that each of us—Mum, Dad, Sean, and I—had recently retired. My brother's body had matured to the point that he was no longer competitive in the endurance sports he'd excelled at in his twenties and thirties. Mum had worked in the special needs community for thirty years, in a job that had required her to do a lot of lifting, which had become too challenging as she got older. Dad had managed a career in the corporate world, and without a high school degree, he'd had to work twice as hard, educating himself at night or at overseas colleges so that he could earn extra degrees. He had more determination than most. He later started a number of small businesses before hitting retirement age and growing weary.

Maybe all four of us were lost.

I couldn't be sure, but I thought Dad probably was—lost with no work of his own to hold on to. And then, all at once, both of his children retired as well. He had become so invested in our dreams, he probably couldn't see where *they* ended and we began. No one knew that state of mind better than I did. He probably feared he was losing everything—losing *us*.

And then we weren't even listening to him: Sean didn't want his help with the career move. I hadn't heeded any of his advice about helping Rafa out of his funk. Perhaps he felt like he was simply fading away, and he was trying to hold on too tightly so he could recapture us again—but instead he'd failed, squashing and suffocating everything, just like Marco had done with the little crab.

It felt like the end of my original family unit as I knew it. And I couldn't see how Dad and I would come back from that fight.

The sun was almost rising when I heard the crackle of

gravel—a car pulling into the driveway. It was Nestor. The car door clicked shut, and his quiet footsteps made their way to our room, where I was awake and crying on the bed. He was shocked to see me there, unable to comprehend how things had gone so wrong in such a short time. His family is Cuban, and though I'd seen some feisty arguments over the years, I'd never seen anything this ferocious.

So he held me, and I finally had a place to fall. Lucky for me, his scenes had finished early and he'd decided to drive home. And I sank into the sweet realization of something I'd already known: Nestor is my home.

We both fell asleep as the sun rose, knowing the boys would be up in a few hours and we needed whatever rest we could get. But that was all I knew. I had no idea what the next hours after that would bring.

In that moment between wakefulness and sleep, I lay in bed and thought about my dad—how he'd charged out after our fight, headed to the beach. I pictured him out roaming in the dark, disheveled and confused. I envisioned him as King Lear, his white hair blowing madly in the wind, completely overcome by his daughter's betrayal, wandering in the thunderstorm and raging against nature.

I awoke to what felt like a chest wound. My imaginary bandages were bloodied, and it hurt to move. Last night . . . it had really happened. My family had fractured. What would happen now?

I had to get out there and face everyone, but the first

moment of this day would be the hardest one. Parents, be they right or wrong, have the ability to reach their children in the deepest caverns of the heart, stripping everything else bare. That morning, I'd be facing my family naked.

What have you ever done with your life?

Those words cut through me again. The wall of dread inside me felt almost insurmountable, but the boys were up and I had to tend to them, so I moved in some sort of forward motion. As I headed out to the kitchen, something occurred to me.

What if Dad didn't even come home last night?

I thought of all that could have happened. Maybe he'd been hurt out there in the dark—he could have tripped on a rock and fallen. In my mind, I saw him clearly: facedown in the sand with a small trickle of blood running from an open wound on the side of his temple.

That kind of imagination is what a life on the stage gets you.

I quickened my pace, and Mum and I collided in the hall-way. Her face was puffy. She looked older, visibly worn in those few short hours.

"I don't know, Shan," she said, shaking her head. She sounded like she had a terrible cold. "It's such a mess. Maybe we should fly home early."

"Where's Dad? Did he come back last night?" I asked anxiously.

"Yes. He's in the kitchen." She sobbed lightly. "He's going to apologize. He feels awful."

"It's okay, Mum. It'll be fine. All families are fucked up," I said, leaning heavily on the word "fucked." I would have hugged her, but I knew she would have fallen apart completely.

I needed to deal with Dad first. So instead, I just patted her back and headed to the kitchen.

Dad was safe. As soon as I'd heard that, my worry had shifted much faster than my brain could track, and now I was incredibly angry—angry deep inside my bones, from my skull all the way to the tips of my toes. Suddenly I didn't even know if I could look at him. I hated him for saying those awful, awful things to me, for playing fast and loose with his power over me. How could he do that? How could he wipe me out like that and diminish my self-worth at the very time I needed it most?

But then I saw him standing at the refrigerator—just the back of him. His tanned legs had become quite bowed in recent years, but his back was still wide and strong, and his chest was still barreled with resolution. When he turned toward me, I saw the deep lines that ran down the corners of his eyes and mouth, and my anger slid into regret.

I'd never really noticed those particular lines before—they seemed to hold all the mistakes he'd made but never admitted to in the past. As he fully faced me, all of my regret just shattered into a sad, painful love. His faded-denim blue eyes looked glassy and swimming with hurt. I couldn't bear it. Seeing him like that made me feel exposed, as if I were stuck on a sandy island all by myself, out in the middle of the ocean, under the hot sun with not one palm tree to shade me. I hated that feeling and looked to him for some kind of relief, some kind of shelter.

"Shan, mate. I am so sorry for what happened last night." His words were clipped, and his diction was formal. I could see this was no small moment in my father's life. Dad was as sincere as I'd ever known him to be; he was speaking from a place of absolute truth. "I'm going to apologize to your brother as well, but I will never forget what I did last night, to the day I die."

I couldn't take it anymore, so I cut him off. I cut the whole thing off. I couldn't match him. I couldn't come from that place deep within.

"It's okay, Dad. It's okay. Don't worry about it."

I wanted to give him more—more time, more space, more understanding, more love. What I really wanted was to ask if there was any truth in that question.

What have you ever done with your life?

But instead, I shriveled. It was just too glaring, too exposed out there without any refuge. I should have gone there. I should have dug to the core of our misunderstanding, walked through the fire with him, and attempted to find our peace. But I shut it all down.

Dad was quick to retreat as well, and we were back in our corners of the ring. I was off the sandy island, and it was over.

Dad apologized to me one more time, on the day he and Mum returned to Australia. I was at the sink doing dishes, and he told me how proud he was of the way I was raising the boys, what good little people they were becoming, and how it was a testament to the care and time both Nestor and I put into being parents. In a graveled tone, he told me he loved me. And I hugged him with wet hands and told him that I knew he did and that everything was okay.

By then, it had already dawned on me what the problem was: I had failed him.

One of the biggest gifts my dad had given me was the freedom to dream. He never put limits on our dreams; we would imagine a future and he'd say, "Why not?" He allowed me to take as many acting and dance classes as I desired, while my brother signed up for as many swim teams and surf club competitions as time would allow. When I said I wanted to study at a drama school in America, Dad didn't hesitate for a moment. Instead he did everything in his power to make it happen. At a time before the internet or Google, he opened up the world for me. Sure, there was other messed-up stuff in my family—we all have our baggage—but in this realm, my dad was the gift giver.

Yet eventually I had denied the gift and walked away from the dream. I'd been defeated by the seeming impossibility of it all, by my inability to do two things at once. Sidetracked by my devotion to motherhood, I had stopped chasing destiny too soon, and somehow this meant I'd betrayed him.

Did he really believe I'd done nothing with my life?

I no longer needed his answer. I saw it now. I'd done some stuff with my life, but ultimately I'd failed him as I'd failed myself. I was him and he was me; over the years, our dream had become one. And I'd been unable to bring it all the way home for him.

After saying goodbye to my parents, I drove back from the airport along the Pali Freeway, which cuts through the dense jungle of the Ko'olau Mountains. It was a rare moment alone, and I was listening to *The Dance* by Fleetwood Mac—a live recording. Right before Stevie Nicks begins the song "Landslide," she says, "This is for you, Daddy." And I began to cry.

What if I had been an iconic rock legend performing to a legion of adoring fans and had been able to dedicate my performance to my dad? And what if he'd been in the audience, and I'd given him that gift—that huge electrifying gift? Would that have made him more satisfied with his life, and me more satisfied with mine? Would great success like that have quieted our demons? Would it have smoothed the conflict between us? Would our fight never have happened?

It was a silly thought—narcissistic and superficial—and I was not proud of it. I was completely aware of how unrealistic and simplistic it was. I was projecting contentment and joy onto two strangers. Yet I continued to indulge my fantasy.

I marveled at the kind of tangible magic Stevie was able to shoot toward her father. I visualized it as a kind of healing ointment, able to clear up all of our wounds. My dad had derived joy from watching me move furniture across a stage, limping all the way with my heel caught in the hem of my skirt. Imagine if I'd made it big; I could've truly blown his mind.

Dad is the sort of guy who loves a little magic. He seems happier when his life has some sparkle around the edges. I was so sorry I wasn't able to give him that—so sorry that in his lifetime, his own greatness wasn't achieved and neither was mine. We'd been able to dream, and we flew a little, but we didn't soar above it all, above the rest. And then we flew back down to the ground. We were, in the end, just humans.

"I'm sorry I failed you," I sobbed, alone in my car.

Stevie rasped out her last few lyrics, the guitar plucked out its finishing notes, the crowd applauded and roared with approval, and I realized what *I* had to do. I had to reconcile with my feelings of failure. I had to bring those feelings on in, live with them, and somehow find a way for them to fit inside me—this *new* me—without tearing me apart. If I could somehow manage to do that, I just might have a chance at not being so lost anymore.

Chapter Eight

AUGUST 2009

Whenever I pack for a vacation, I place an outfit in my suitcase that I've never worn in my day-to-day life. It's usually something that has been hanging in my closet, tags still attached—an outfit I had loved in the store, but when I tried it on back at home, it didn't feel like me. On vacation, I reason, I'm not at home. I am a stranger in a new land, so I can reinvent myself. I can be anyone I want to be—a freer, better me. Yet despite this hopeful ritual, more often than not, the outfit comes back in the suitcase with the tags still attached, unworn, and returned to the store.

In Hawaii, after Mum, Dad, Sean, and Sal left—all the witnesses to the big fight—I had the urge to put on one of those outfits. I figured out what I had to do: I had to fully reconcile with myself—a better me who was free from the shackles of my past as an "also ran" actress.

I was the wife of Nestor, who was on Oʻahu to work as an actor on *LOST*. I was the mom of Rafa and Marco, who would be in school for a year in Hawaii while their dad worked. And I was me—just me—a woman who was new in town. I wouldn't be meeting a whole lot of actors on the island. I wouldn't be confronted by my past, my shortcomings, my longevity as an actress. It was a perfect place to just settle in and do what I needed to do, be who I needed to be. In other words, it was the perfect place to wear an outfit that had been waiting for me in my closet.

I had one big problem, though: My body was starting to betray me. Every time I remembered the fight—what my dad had said, what I'd said back to him—I could feel myself beginning to rattle on the inside. I'd get short of breath, my muscles would tighten, and I'd panic.

The panic would then escape the confines of that memory and spill over into every aspect of our new life on the island. All the steps we'd taken to get things going—searching for a pediatrician, meeting administrators at the new schools, signing the boys up for swimming lessons, even finding a Target to buy them school supplies—had brought on panic. How on earth was I going to help the boys transition, establish a sense of normalcy, and put on the frickin' outfit when I was gasping for air and trying to stop myself from visibly trembling?

I still hadn't let go of my anger toward Dad, and I could barely keep up with the pendulum swing of my own emotions. He had behaved badly the night of the fight, but I had come to a kind of peace with it soon after he left. I understood him. I saw for a minute where he was coming from and my own culpability in the fight. But then . . . I'd start to shake, to panic, and I hated him all over again. He had come and gone, leaving me as wreckage on the beach.

LOST was also on my mind. With Nestor working on scripts and the locations right there in front of me, I began to feel like one of the survivors of Oceanic Flight 815. My plane had suffered a midair breakup, crashed on an unidentifiable island, and left me stranded. I had to "go back," like the characters on *LOST*—back to my original self, before all the shaking started, before all of my big dreams had taken root. But I knew no way of getting there.

One afternoon toward the end of August, as Nestor, the boys, and I were driving to Longs Drugs in Kailua Town to set up our prescription accounts, a familiar, uncomfortable feeling came over me.

"I'm out of breath again," I said softly to Nestor.

"Try that yoga breathing thing," he suggested.

A therapist had taught it to me when I'd had panic attacks before. You cover one nostril and breathe in for seven seconds, then cover the other nostril and let the breath out for seven seconds. It helped a bit, but I'd much rather take a pill that really worked. I had taken Ativan before, but it was a controlled substance that could not be prescribed in one state and filled in another. I'd have to find a doctor, explain my history, request the medicine, and hope the doctor would give it to me. That entire process seemed more complicated than white-knuckling it.

"Look, Mom, there's the mystery storefront," Rafa called from the back seat, pointing to an establishment that had no visible storefront or even a sign out front. Despite this, there was always a long line of people waiting on the sidewalk to get in, making this store something of a mystery to us. The boys and I always took this route on our way to Foodland for grocery shopping. I had waffled between guessing it was the location of a youth church group meeting to thinking it might be an unemployment center. Rafa never faltered in his belief that it was a pinball palace, and I loved his conviction.

This time, his comment distracted me and instantly pulled me out of my panic attack. At times, kids can be God's medicine.

We went into Longs and up to the pharmacy counter. The lovely woman there was all smiles. She recognized Nestor from TV, talked about all the different shows she'd seen him in, and welcomed us to Kailua and the island. The production of *LOST* had brought a great deal of pride to the people of O'ahu, and the cast was treated kindly. Whenever people recognized Nestor, they invariably mentioned another cast member who also lived in town, telling us how nice the person was, or shared with us little details from their lives, such as what they'd come into town to shop for.

But as the Longs lady started to enter our prescription information, her warm smile faded. She looked up at me sadly and then started to smile at me in a different way, as if to say, *You poor thing. You are unhappy. Even in paradise!*

She had read my prescription, of course. It was for a common antidepressant—not even a particularly large dose—so there was no real need for alarm. I wasn't about to bite down on rubber or anything. But as she looked at me with such sympathy, the town of Kailua suddenly felt stiflingly small.

❀

Perhaps I've always been a depressive person, but I'd known of my acute depression since the age of twenty-seven, when I gained a very clear understanding of myself. Ever since I'd walked away from acting, I'd been indulging in some self-reflection, kind of like the chicken-or-egg dilemma: Did I become an actress because I was a depressive? Or did I become a depressive as the result of being an actress—an actress who was never able to take rejection lightly, no matter how much I rationalized it as simply the nature of the business I was in?

And then there was the big question: Had I not been a depressive, would I have been a more successful actress?

As a young girl, I fantasized about being a foreign exchange student in an American high school just like Rydell High from the movie *Grease*. I said my prayers every night, asking God to transport me to the world of whatever novel I was reading at the time—be it dark or light. I wanted to smell the air . . . ramble through the landscape . . . soak in every lane, bridge, valley, and tunnel . . . and of course, kiss the boy. I loved the idea of living in a foreign place, be it imaginary or real. And then I moved to America.

It would be romantic to surmise I was a born adventurer, an explorer, but I think I was a runner. And the problem was I was yearning for an escape from my own internal emotional storm, although at the beginning it was more of an unstable weather pattern.

Even as a little girl, I felt things in a very big way. I remember a day when my mum was a little late to pick me up from ballet class. I must've been around seven years old. I was waiting outside of the community center alone, and it was getting dark. I don't recall what I thought had happened to her—only that I somehow convinced myself I'd never see her again. I cried so hard I made myself vomit.

I have another memory of lying in the back seat while my dad was driving our car. He had just returned from a long business trip, and I'd talked myself into believing the man driving along the road was not my dad but an imposter who looked and sounded exactly like him and intended to do us some kind of harm. As I lay there in the moving car, genuinely frightened, I tried to hatch an escape plan.

So perhaps the writing was already on the wall. I had always put my body through a load of unnecessary emotional turmoil and stress. But I made it to twenty-seven before I felt *the click*, and then everything changed—and not for the better.

It was as though there were little buckets in my brain that were delicately balanced, until one suddenly capsized. As it capsized, I slipped on the chemicals leaking from that bucket, down into a well that felt like it was made of liquid metal. And from deep inside that well, everything was different. The tiniest moments of the day that used to bring me just a small amount of pleasure were still happening, but I could feel nothing. Meanwhile, the big, hard parts of life were overwhelming and inescapably sad.

I did my best to claw my way out of that well, but the molten metal made it impossible to find a grip. I asked God to help me escape, swearing I'd ask for nothing else ever again. Climbing out of that well, for me, was like holding on to life itself.

I'd fallen into a true chemical depression. One therapist told Nestor and me that we'd survive as a couple only if he were willing to accept that mine was the mind of a little girl, and that he'd have to nurture me like a father and show the patience of a parent until I recovered.

Fuck that, I thought, and I went to a different doctor, who prescribed a combination of medicine and therapy. Nestor was a young man, my boyfriend of only a year, and I couldn't expect him to take on the role of father to a grown woman. I took the medicine and went to therapy, and eventually I was able to relaunch my life from what felt much more like a flat, even playing field.

Thank goodness I live in an age of psychotropic medicine—and I was able to avoid a mental institution—but there is still a stigma attached to depression and taking antidepressants. It's certainly not something most people put out into the world, like "I have diabetes" or "I have a low-functioning thyroid." So as the Longs lady looked at me with such sympathy, I had the feeling she'd been right outside our house on the night of the "fuck you" fight with my dad, and she'd heard everything.

⚜

I tried smiling blandly like I'd just handed over a prescription for an antihistamine or an antibiotic. But underneath my smile, I was screaming.

Listen, lady, you seem disappointed, but this is all I've got now. The mountains and the ocean and the five million different colors of the sun rising and setting are amazing, but they're not doing it for me. These pills are the only thing holding me together, and they are just barely working. In fact, if you could throw in some Xanax or a little Ativan, I'd be so grateful, because I'm shaking like a leaf and I don't know how long this deep breathing thing will work.

I'm going through some shit that might seem pretty frickin' stupid to you. I get it. It's narcissistic, and I hate that. But you know what isn't stupid? I'm a mother, and a mother cannot fall into a true depression. Not the depression I was in before I started on these pills. Because if I fall into that place again—that place down the steel well, where my only escape was to leave or take medicine, and I'm already on medicine—then I'm truly screwed. My boys will have no hope, because I will not be able to be their mother.

And I cannot leave them. They do not deserve to have their lives rattled by this defect in my brain. They are good and sweet, and I'd miss them like a lung would miss oxygen, and they'd miss me, just not as much. So I am pretty un-fucking-happy in Hawaii, but that's okay, the pills will help and I'll work on the rest. So please fill that prescription, and I'll be back in a few days for pickup.

As we turned to leave, I summoned my actual voice, which came out like a squeaky whisper: "Oh, and I'd prefer not to have the generic medicine. The real stuff works better for me. Thanks so much." And we left.

The next day, my phone rang. It was the Longs lady, calling me because she was worried she might have offended me.

Oh no.

Did she notice *I* noticed the change of expression on her face? Were we about to have an awkward conversation about my depression—about how it started? A wave of fear washed over me. I suddenly wondered if I'd actually said out loud all the stuff in my head. I felt jet-lagged and became momentarily confused: *Where am I? How did I get here? Or am I just dreaming?*

I started to sweat, and I longed for our old Los Angeles Rite Aid, where the pharmacy people just handed over our prescriptions with a quick exchange about the weather.

"I just didn't want you to feel bad," she continued kindly, "because I see you've really worked on a lot of different things, too." She felt bad about recognizing Nestor the day before and not me.

Though slightly mortified and somewhat confused, I told her it truly wasn't a big deal, I was not the least bit offended, and I actually enjoyed it when people recognized Nestor.

"I'm really more of a mom now, anyway," I added, and we said our goodbyes.

After we hung up, I realized we had not talked about my prescriptions at all. The only reason she had called was to talk to me about my acting—as though she was on a one-woman mission to make me happy, to validate my life and career. Yet the thing she thought would make me happy was the very thing I was attempting to push away, to separate from myself while I was in Hawaii.

I was embarrassed by her kindness; from anyone else it would have felt unfamiliar and affronting, too. But she had a beautiful way about her, and somehow I didn't mind talking about my career. In fact, the phone call made me happy.

Nonetheless, when I slunk in a few days later to pick up my medicine, I was really hoping not to see my new pharmacy friend. I was out of luck; she was there. But as I waited in line, I really started to *see* her: her clear brown skin. The beautiful, wide planes of her face. Her shiny, cherry-like cheekbones. Her perfectly plucked eyebrows. Her nametag said she was Patty.

As I waited, I heard her speak with the same kind of care and concern to the person in front of me, who was talking freely and laughing while interacting with her. I realized Patty was simply kind and curious and open. She had no agenda to make me happy in Hawaii; she was just being Patty. She had no investment in my success or failure as an actress. She saw it as a part of me, but not the whole me. Like all the customers who came in, I was an individual with a life and a heart. We were all individuals, and who we became in her presence was a reflection of her actions. Because she was genuine, people were authentic and easy when they were with her.

When I reached the counter, I could not keep myself from grinning. What a gift she was! Patty smiled really big in return. I had to push some tears down, lest she think I was a super-duper head case. She gave me my meds, and I thanked her. As I walked away, I could hear her kind voice addressing the next customer. I hurried out of there before I exploded with emotion. I hadn't been able to get back to who I was before my shaking started, before I let go of my dreams. And in that moment Patty became my guide.

Back in the parking lot, my phone dinged. Two other *LOST* actors' wives had texted to see if I was available for lunch or coffee. My first instinct was to shy away from such an invitation, but then I realized I'd be able to accept it. I could manage it without shaking, because I'd learned something from Patty. Patty saw me as complete. She saw my wholeness. I didn't have to re-create myself or forget who I used to be just because I'd failed at my dream.

I had experienced myself as a reflection of what Patty saw in me. I could tell she liked me, just as much as I liked her. I didn't feel the need to hide who I used to be. Even though the inhales still hurt—especially when I thought about the big roles I almost booked or saw other actresses who'd landed those roles—I could attempt to exhale away the pain. I could try to free myself of the weight that came with those old agendas. I didn't need to wear the outfit I'd packed as a tool to reinvent myself. My impulse now favored stripping down to the real me, with all of my history (good and bad) and an open acceptance of who I was because of it.

I sighed with relief as the balance shifted slightly toward the good, and I silently thanked Patty for that.

Chapter Nine

AUGUST 2009

I t was early evening, and the Hawaiian trade winds were up, blowing hard off the ocean and sneaking through the cracks under the doors and the louvered vents on the front windows. The wind in our Kailua house was beginning to feel like a fifth member of our family—alive, talkative, constantly demanding to be felt and heard. It reminded me we were transplants, unfamiliar yet committed to our new life in the tropics. LA County seems to get breezy only when the Santa Ana winds blow in with their blustery, dry heat. We had made a shift, and I loved the idea that we had picked up and moved ourselves to somewhere so exotic.

As I passed the boys' bedroom on the way to my own, a small hand gripped my arm. It was Rafa. He yanked me into his room, closed the door, and sat me on his bed. "I've changed my mind," he quickly confessed. "I don't want to go to my new school after all."

My stomach dropped to the floor.

Tomorrow was the first day of school, and Rafa clearly wasn't reveling in the idea of our shift like I had been. A few days earlier, at the "meet the teacher" morning, he'd loved his classroom and just being there at the school—so much that he didn't want to leave. But he had been assessing things since then, and he'd figured it out: At school, he was going to be alone, completely isolated from any human being whom he knew (or who knew him), for six and three-quarters of an hour. I'd wondered if and when this fact would hit him, and I couldn't blame him. After all, he was only seven years old.

I'd set up a playdate for him with the son of one of the *LOST* actors, but the little boy was not in his class. At the meeting, we'd learned the classes ate lunch and had recess at different times. Not that it mattered—Rafa wouldn't have looked for this boy on the playground. They were both shy kids and hadn't really bonded. I should have asked for a class list earlier and set up more playdates.

I'd really dropped the ball.

We sat on the edge of his little wood-frame bed, on a faded orange Hawaiian quilt softened by hundreds of washes. I explained to Rafa that changing his mind was perfectly normal, because he was anxious. I reassured him we were all a little scared about not really knowing anybody here in Hawaii. Marco walked into the bedroom just then, prompting me to remark on how he was also a bit frightened and had even started developing a few nervous habits.

Marco froze, locking eyes with me. I began to regret throwing my innocent four-year-old under the bus.

"What are my nervous habits?" Marco asked me with wide eyes.

"Well," I said apprehensively, "you've been, umm . . . kind of coughing or clearing your throat a lot lately. And, well . . . you sort of make a whinny sound like a horse when you become frustrated. Kind of like this—"

I demonstrated the *brrrrrr* noise he'd developed as a nervous tic.

There was silence as I waited, dreading his response while imagining a psychiatrist slapping me on the wrist. But all of a sudden, Marco clapped his hands with glee.

"I have two habits!" he declared.

"Well, actually you have three!" I went on, buoyed by his response. "You also blink a lot when you're anxious!"

"I have *three* habits," he bragged to his brother. He couldn't have been happier.

"Do I have a nervous habit?" Rafa asked me tentatively.

Nestor and I had both noticed Rafa had developed a really loud, forced guffaw after everything he himself perceived as funny. But I didn't have the heart to revel in his nerdy quirk.

"Not really . . . but I have one," I said. "I've started picking all the dead skin off my scalp!" I immediately regretted sharing this gross fact, yet I still went on. "I can't stop picking it. I'm picking it all the time. Sometimes I pick it until it bleeds!"

Why am I telling them this? What is wrong with me?

I reasoned to myself it was better than telling them Mommy had begun shaking and gasping for air because she'd failed at her big dream—walked away from it because the two of them were born. Yes, it was better to go with my scalp-picking habit.

So I told them I'd developed a dry scalp because of all the swimming we'd been doing, and I'd been picking at my head until scabs had formed.

"Yay! You have a habit too, Mama," Marco squealed.

Rafa just looked at me with a mix of confusion and horror, so I decided to change the subject.

As I readied him for bed, I assured him he was an easy kid to get along with. Kids would want to be his friend immediately, and in just five minutes his nerves would go away. It was normal to be nervous, I explained, and I'd worry about him more if he wasn't nervous or had zero apprehension. That was a lie.

I *was* worried about him. A boulder of worry had already begun to form on my chest, and I started to do my yoga breathing in a very subtle way, as though I were just playing around with my nose. He was going to be lonely for hours on end, and I had a feeling time went by more slowly in a little person's world. I knew what it was like to be lonely—completely alone with no familiar soul to turn to. I knew that feeling intimately, and I remembered those days, those hours, those minutes with exact and excruciating detail.

❀

A few days after I graduated high school, I was cast in an Australian prime-time soap opera called *Sons and Daughters.* Though I was grateful for the job, working professionally only reinforced my instincts that I needed formal training as an actor. Sometimes my scenes would work, and sometimes they wouldn't—and I'd have no idea why.

I decided to study theater at California Institute of the Arts. The money I earned from the soap opera would pay for my whole first year abroad. I was eighteen when I arrived in America with four heavy suitcases, a backpack, and an acoustic guitar in a worn-out traveling case. A good guy I'd met just before I left Australia had given me the guitar case as a parting gift. When I'd tried to refuse his kindness, he told me I'd need it more than he would.

"I'm not going anywhere anytime soon," he'd said with certainty. He was fresh out of drama school and had started working with some high-quality theater companies. He expressed no desire for notoriety, although in the years to come, local fame would find him, and I'm sure he didn't hate it.

My brother had some producer friends who lived in Hollywood. He'd met them Down Under while they were doing research on a movie about the Australian surf lifesaving world. They had a small house on the outskirts of Korea Town and had agreed to let me stay in their guesthouse before the semester started. I couldn't afford a cab from the airport, so the plan was to catch the LAX Speedy Shuttle that made a drop at the Hollywood Roosevelt Hotel, call them from the pay phone in the lobby, and wait for them to pick me up from there. It was 1987, and there were no cell phones.

The shuttle deposited me in the middle of Hollywood Boulevard, right in front of the hotel. As I climbed down the bus steps, the driver unloaded my four bags neatly in a row on the sidewalk. I paid him (minus the tip—a custom I'd learn in time), and then he was gone.

Now, away from the airport and no longer inside a moving vehicle, I could take in the city of Hollywood for the first time. I had to shield my eyes; it was hot and bright. Los Angeles has a special kind of light—a tone flat and even (although back then I would have called it "glaring"). Blocking out the sun with my hand, I saw a whole slew of what my mother would call "unsavory" people weaving in and out of the hundreds of tourists, who were distinctly dressed in midthigh shorts and long T-shirts embellished with animated characters or catch-phrases. The steady stream of cars on the boulevard made everything loud. Not the assault of a honking, yelling, and screeching of brakes—Sydney City loud—but more like a jet engine, a constant rumble in the background.

The noise intensified my dilemma and made it difficult to concentrate. How was I going to get into the hotel to make the call with my four bags, my guitar case, and my backpack? Carrying all my stuff at once was a physical impossibility. It was a riddle: I'd be stranded if I didn't make the call, but making the call meant leaving at least half of my worldly possessions unattended on the sidewalk.

I stood helplessly on the street, trying to figure out the vibe. Although it seemed like a dodgy part of town, all those tourists looked unthreatening, albeit distracted. It was the mix that confused me: the bad element alongside those who were just trying to see the town, to check out Hollywood. Why were the innocent tourists hanging around with the hustlers-who-were-perhaps-drug-addicts? In Sydney, the neighborhoods were much more segregated, with good neighborhoods set apart from the bad. And in my little northern beach town, we were set apart from pretty much everything—no tourists *or* shady people.

As I stood for a little while longer, an unsettling chill coursed through my body. I had lived eighteen years and had never felt anything like it: complete solitude and isolation. Standing on that crowded sidewalk in the bright sunlight, I was truly alone for the first time. I'd left everyone I knew, let alone everyone I loved. I'd been hyper focused on going to school—wherever that might be—to better myself as an actress so I could become a big movie star. It had never crossed my mind I'd be throwing myself into absolute desolation. My current circumstance made this situation undeniable. All I had to do was make a phone call, but I was just one person, completely alone . . . and I had no way of managing it.

Had I been standing there a little too long? Probably. Some of the shady people were eyeballing me in a predatory way. My instincts told me I needed to make a move fast, lest I become their next meal. One man in particular was watching me—he was definitely not a tourist, but he didn't look high on drugs either. He was balding, but the yellow-blond hair that remained at the front of his scalp looked unnatural and porous at the roots. He seemed more smarmy than dangerous, so I made the calculated decision to ask for his help.

"Excuse me?" I said.

He was surprised when I spoke to him.

"Can I ask you the biggest favor? Do you think you could help me get two of these bags into the hotel foyer? I can manage the rest on my own."

I'd taken him off guard. He hesitated and then said, "Yes," before hauling two of my insanely heavy suitcases inside.

"Thank you so much. That was so nice of you," I said sweetly, in the hopes he'd then promptly leave. But he didn't. He just stayed there in the hotel foyer and sort of watched me, openly assessing my every move.

I had come prepared with American quarters to make the phone call for my ride, but this took much longer than I'd anticipated. For the life of me, I could not decipher what the automated lady was talking about.

Should I put the quarter in before I dial . . . or after?

Do I dial the area code or the number "one" first?

Or do I not dial the number "one" at all?

I reinserted that frickin' quarter about fifty times, all while scanning my suitcases, wiping sweat out of my eyes, and keeping tabs on whether the man was still watching me. He was. But I pretended not to know he was there. I finally hit the lucky number and got a hold of my brother's friend, who promised to be there in about fifteen minutes.

Fifteen whole minutes?

I wasn't sure if I could hold off the smarmy man for that long.

I kept talking into the phone long after my brother's friend hung up, until that *If you'd like to make a call, please hang up and try again* message repeated so often and so loudly I was sure everyone around me had caught on to my act—especially my creepy guy, who was still silently enjoying the show. So I hung up nonchalantly and pulled my bags into me like a low-walled castle fortress.

When he finally began to talk to me, I feigned a small gasp

of mild shock, as if to say, *You're still here?* He wasn't overly cheerful or incredibly serious, just very direct and almost studious as he attempted to get a read on me. He crept in closer and started to pepper me with questions, which I answered politely but cautiously.

I'm here to go to theater school . . .

I'm staying with friends . . .

I'm from Australia . . .

And so on and so on. To my relief, my ride finally arrived.

As I left, the man handed me a business card, telling me he was a manager and he'd love to represent me as an actress. He assured me he knew everyone in town. I may have been from a small beach town in Australia, but I knew how that story would end. Yet his words—"I could make things very easy for you"—sounded very appealing.

Against all my good instincts, I paused to consider his offer. *What if he just happened to be the one person on Hollywood Boulevard who was legitimate?* But after a moment, I remembered reading a paragraph in our acting curriculum package, which I quickly recited back to him: "Oh yes. Yeah, we're not allowed to do any kind of outside work until at least our second year of theater school, so I'd better not. Thank you so much, though. Bye."

Then I hurried on, wondering if I'd walked away from a lost opportunity. A few minutes later, he was out of my mind.

What did stick, lingering around the edges of my consciousness for years, was that intense moment on the sidewalk of Hollywood Boulevard when the realization hit: I had orchestrated a life for myself that called for complete isolation from all the people I knew in the world.

My four years at CalArts were nothing like an American kid imagines their college experience to be. They were fulfilling years, but not happy ones. The school was small, with only twenty actors in my graduating class. Most of my American classmates were fresh out of high school—binge drinking, hooking up, and reveling in their newly found freedom—whereas I had been working, living away from home, and going to bars and parties for quite some time in Australia already. I became good friends with some of the older students, many of whom were in relationships and had cars and enough money to get off campus. I had no car nor any money to spare. I dated a little, but either culture shock, the dating pool at a small, quirky art school, or just being preoccupied with my own pain management prevented me from getting serious with any guys.

Instead, I devoted myself to learning. Aside from my studio class productions, I signed up to be in every student film or experimental theater piece I could. I was like an apprentice painter who'd made the journey to Renaissance Europe to learn from the masters. I worked and worked, developing characters on weekends so I could bring them into rehearsals with my classmates on Mondays. I suffered the agony of loneliness, much like a ballerina suffers blisters on her toes from wearing pointe shoes. And I became a strong girl who could stand solidly on her own.

But I was just so sad, so much of the time. I wrote letter after letter back home. One particular letter to my friend Kerrie contained a revelation of sorts, something I'd never even pondered before: I had discovered it was possible to be on one's own. It was really awful and hard, but amazing in a way—and now that I'd learned how, I'd never have to settle for a guy I wasn't completely in love with.

But the truth was, loneliness had taken a toll on me. Something in me had altered—too much sadness had been piled onto one side. I used to laugh so much in Australia, with my family and my relatives and especially my girl-friends. The people around me were mostly easygoing, and my young, tiny, lucky little world was a jovial place. I was a blessed person, bawdy and fun. I laughed with my friends until I couldn't breathe. I'm sure I laughed with my CalArts classmates, too, but I never laughed when I was alone. And I was alone so often in those four years that my laughter really died off.

Was it all worth it? I wondered, lying beside Rafa on the orange Hawaiian quilt the night before the first day of school. *Was the solitude worth the pursuit of my dream? Was the joy lost in those four years worth the steps I took forward as an actress?*

Rafa had finally drifted to sleep. I looked at his pale scapula bone next to my arm and the tip of his diminutive shoulder peeking out from under the quilt. The frailty of his small body set my heart beating in an irregular pattern. I pictured him in school the next day among rows of children's faces, the soft light bouncing off the beautiful angles of his cheekbones and the sharp jawline he'd inherited from Nestor. Rafa always looked to me like he was blinking in slow motion. His world-weary brow and translucent, almost pale-blue skin were made for French films.

Then I imagined his black lashes lifting slowly to reveal his deep, complicated eyes and his sad little face. His face was too young to look that sad. He was too young to be in front of the Hollywood Roosevelt Hotel with all that baggage, not knowing another soul.

※

We moved around the house that next morning with silent resolve. The day was so scary for Rafa, it just seemed sacrilegious to force any kind of cheer. His new school, Le Jardin Academy, had been built on the site of the former Kailua drive-in movie theater right at the foot of the Koʻolau Range, overlooking the Kawainui Marsh. The marsh is eight hundred acres of wet meadow behind a serpentine flood levee Nestor affectionately called "the Great Wall of Kailua." It was not unusual to see chickens and bush turkeys on the side of the road as we drove up to school. On lucky days, we'd see wild boars, and on extra-lucky days, even a baby boar.

That first morning, the small classroom was hot and crowded with parents attempting to make their kids comfortable. I was mostly focused on Rafa, of course, but I did notice a boy coming out of the bathroom, wiping tears from his cheeks with the heels of his hands and then rubbing them dry on his shorts. He was a tall boy with mousy brown hair, light golden skin, and bright blue eyes. He was missing a tooth on each side of his two front ones, and he looked as American as Rafa did not. He wasn't with his mom or dad, and as he slipped self-consciously into the seat behind his desk, I could see he didn't want to be noticed.

The teacher announced it was time for the parents to leave, and my body twitched at the sound of her voice. Rafa grabbed hold of my hand and pleaded a soft "no" to me with his chin down and his eyes like laser beams, penetrating mine. Tears were forming, though he was willing them not to drop. But we had to leave.

Loosening my hand out of his tight grip—when all I wanted to do was grab him and run—was almost too hard to bear. As my flesh left his, the misery of separation sliced through me, as deep as any cut or burn. All I could do was pray Rafa didn't feel it too. As he took his seat, I was happy to see he had been placed next to the tall boy with the missing teeth. His name sticker read: *Joey.*

"Rafa, this is Joey. Joey, this is Rafa," I said, just as the teacher all but pushed me out of the door. All I could do was hope the two boys might bond in their despair.

"Did you see that big boy was also crying? Joey?" I whimpered to Nestor through my own tears as we drove away from the school.

"Yes," he replied. "His dad is in the army. Just deployed to Afghanistan two days ago."

Nestor had been talking to Joey's mom, who had left early to settle her younger daughter into class. Her husband, a head and neck surgeon, had just left to do an eight-month tour in Bagram. Even though Joey had been at the school since kindergarten, she explained, he was feeling fragile.

"Oh, that poor kid," I said. "He was trying so hard not to cry."

"Yeah," agreed Nestor. "His mom seemed really nice."

As we headed along the Pali Freeway toward our house, I looked out the window and thought about Joey, who looked so shaky even on familiar ground. Surely nobody was sharing their worries about his dad—in fact, most likely the opposite.

He'd have no clue that his father had just been sent to the most dangerous place on earth. But eight months without your dad is daunting under any circumstances, and a seven-year-old understands the basic concept of war, no matter how it's spun.

In addition to worrying about Rafa that day, my mind was heavy with thoughts of Joey.

Since becoming a mother, I feel the hurt of boy-pain in an especially profound way. When I experienced pain as a young girl, I somehow managed to plow through the hurt head-on and come out mostly intact. I witnessed my little girlfriends doing the same. I'm not sure my boys can do that. I don't think they have the pain-management skills we girls had at their age. I see them suffer an emotional injury but quickly cover by looking down or away. I know Nestor and I can guide them through the healthy steps to find relief, but it's the seconds between the hurt and the cover—those moments when they are truly at a loss for how to cope—it's *that* space that kills me. Those lost moments when they are stranded makes me want to run and fall on their swords if need be.

I was still thinking about Rafa and Marco (and Joey too) when I took my first Hawaiian bike ride. I had bought a hybrid bike from the Kailua Bike Shop and justified the cost as equal to a year's gym membership. My plan was to ride my bike around our side of the island—my new workout routine. Nestor persuaded me to go, reminding me my self-imposed start date was Rafa's first day of school. I needed to get out and get started.

I left our street and headed down Kalaheo Avenue, the main beach road in Kailua. I hit Kailua Beach Park and started to cross the bridge that runs over the Kawainui Canal, which runs out from the marsh to the ocean. Sand constantly blows up from the beach onto this part of the bike path, making it really, really slippery—skating-on-oil-covered-ice slippery. When I rode over it too fast, I lost control, skidded, and fell onto my side. My bike landed on top of me.

A few onlookers stopped and gasped. Suddenly, I was grateful to know so few people in town. I wanted to melt away, but instead I just brushed myself off quickly and smiled, declaring I was fine. Then I jumped back on my bike and kept riding. My leg was pretty scraped up, but I was okay. Lesson learned: Never ride fast on a sandy path. Or if you do, just get up and pretend everything is fine. Chances are, minutes after you declare everything's good, it generally will be. I wanted Rafa to be resilient like that.

But the truth was, everything was not good. Although I'd been trying to pretend the hole in my chest was fine, it just wouldn't go away.

I rode up the hill and down into Lanikai, a neighborhood on a smaller, more serene beach. The beauty of the coast was stunning, but my heart and mind were not really present or able to drink it all in. They were still with my boy.

Only when Rafa was safely encapsulated in my minivan that afternoon did I experience some relief. "So? Did you love it, like it, or hate it?" I asked.

"I liked it," Rafa answered, his tone straightforward and even.

Well, he isn't jumping for the stars, I thought. But nor did he seem completely miserable. It was a start.

One of my mentors at CalArts, who was also a movement

and centering teacher, once gave me advice. I worked as her teaching assistant, and she came to see me in every play I was in. One morning, after she'd seen me in a play the night before, I lamented that my previous performance had been better. My teacher just nodded silently—her usual cup of coffee in one hand and cigarette in the other. She sucked in the last of her cigarette, threw the butt in her coffee, and placed the cup on the floor. Then she began to align my posture with her hands.

"Shannon, no breath we take is like the last one," she said, widening my shoulders. "No minute is like the last minute. No day is like the last day." She was rolling my head in circles at this point. "So how can one performance be like the last performance? Don't set up those comparisons in your mind. Don't take control when you should be letting go."

Her response bummed me out. I wanted her to say that I was wrong, that in fact I was brilliant in the play, that I'd become a great actress and a star.

"I don't know what you'll do with your life, but I do know you're growing into an artist," my mentor assured me as she wound up our conversation.

Despite my solitude, I learned so many truisms like that at CalArts, where I had nothing else to do but sponge up every wise thing my teachers taught me. I eventually learned to trust in my work and myself, and now I recognized the incredible value in my mentor's advice.

No day is like the last day. No year is like the last year.

Rafa's year didn't have to mirror my years of intense loneliness.

As it turned out, much of what I learned had very little to

do with becoming a movie star and a whole lot more to do with being a creative soul—and perhaps a better person. So it seemed I had an answer after all: Those four years of solitude *were* worth it. They had been painful but meaningful too. To what active purpose, of course, I still had no idea.

If I knew that, I surmised, *I'd be a whole lot less lost.*

But the strong feeling I had about those years being not only worthwhile but profound in so many ways made me feel . . . a bit more found.

"I met a new friend," Rafa continued, snapping me back to the here and now in our minivan in Kailua. "Joey. We want to have a playdate. Can you please call his mom?"

"You bet your boots!" I replied, way too enthusiastically.

I looked at the class phone list and texted Joey's mom, Barbara, right away. My phone dinged back almost immediately. Barb welcomed me to town and said they'd love to set up a playdate. Joey had come back from his first day of school declaring he'd met a new boy, Rafa, who was now his very best friend.

Barb's next text made me laugh: "I only hope he doesn't give his heart to a girl that quickly."

I marveled that she'd just seen her husband off to war and seemed to be in such good humor. I looked forward to meeting her and to seeing how Rafa's year would unfold. And I had a strong feeling he would be okay.

It was all progress.

Chapter Ten

SEPTEMBER 2009

As a little girl, every day I walked on a sacred piece of the earth, and I never told another soul of its power. I named it Prayer Hill, and of course, I was the only one who deemed it sacred. I wasn't a peaceful child; my emotions were constantly churning, and I sometimes felt outside of myself, looking in. But Prayer Hill was my anchor.

Thirty years later, my head was still churning, and often I was still hovering above myself. I had other anchors—Nestor and the boys—but no internal grounding force like I'd found on Prayer Hill. And if there was ever a time I needed one, it was during those years just after I quit acting.

Until I was twelve years old, my family lived in a little suburb called Elanora Heights: "Elanora" from the Aboriginal for "home by the sea," and "Heights" for the hill on which the town sits. My two childhood girlfriends Jenny and

Katrina also lived there—next door to each other a little farther in from my house, which was built on a cul-de-sac at the edge of town. We'd always walk home together from school or after playing around the neighborhood. I'd say goodbye to them and continue along their street and then up a small incline that led into my avenue. The roads were so quiet, I'd walk right in the middle of the asphalt and never on the grass; there were no sidewalks, and I was always alone. Dogs ran unleashed in those days, so the likelihood of stepping on poop in the grass was high.

Prayer Hill was tiny, but all I could see as I climbed was the black of the road and, once I reached the top, nothing but miles of green and grey-blue bush from the valley down below. As I descended, I'd try to see if I could glimpse a part of Narrabeen Lagoon in the valley floor, to find it glistening between the rooftops along the ridge. Then I'd round a corner to reach my house, and on this small section of my journey, I'd always—without fail—talk to God.

I was raised Catholic. I had my share of snarky scripture teachers who put the fear of God in me about failing to communicate with, well . . . God. We also had an old-school parish priest—the kind who bellowed through his sermon, admonishing all the sinners who weren't at Mass, which was ironic because he was preaching to the ones who *were* at Mass.

I was mostly an obedient child, however, who honored our church elders. I hated to be in trouble in general, so being in trouble with *God* would be a burden too heavy for my conscience. Naturally, I was riddled with guilt and unable to take God for granted, so I got into the habit of talking to him often, especially when I didn't need anything from him (just like we'd been told to do). Prayer Hill was my own reminder to say hi to God, to check in and say, *Thank you.*

And it worked. I prayed on that hill almost every day. I remember feeling connected to God in those years. But Prayer Hill had faded from my memory long ago—until the day in Hawaii when I found myself hiking with Angel.

∗

I had never met Angel—had no idea who she even was—until the day of the hike. Our real estate agent, upon hearing the boys had started school, thoughtfully invited me on a hike with a group of women. My first instinct was to say no. It was hard to summon the courage to mingle with a woman I barely knew and six of her best girlfriends. The anxiety attacks that had started after the fight with Dad were still a problem. They were triggered by specific events—like school pickup and drop-off.

I used to audition fifteen-page scenes in rooms with thirty-odd network executives after signing off on test deals that were potentially worth more than I'd ever made in a year, but now I was somehow terrified of my kid's elementary school carpool. Unfortunately, Rafa's campus was the very spot where the women would park and gather so we could all ride together to the site of the hike. How much easier it would be to decline the invitation. I didn't want to face that spot on the map.

But I'd learned from Patty at Longs Drugs that I could take in a new person, and with no agenda. Staying true to that task required being there, breath by breath, in the moment. If I did that, there'd be no time for the shakes to set in.

Besides, a lot of women were going. *I won't have to get incredibly deep with any one person,* I told myself. And really, what kind of chickenshit forces her kids to meet new people and make new friends when she doesn't have the fortitude to do it herself?

So I said, "Yes, I'd love to," and was soon added to the text thread.

The night before the hike, six of the women (including our real estate agent) pulled out for one reason or another. That left two of us still standing: me and a lady named Angel.

This is worse than awkward, I thought. *This is terrifying.*

When Angel chimed in to say she was still game if I was (which was incredibly gracious of her), I was tempted to stay curled up in my bed the following morning, solitary and safe. But instead I texted:

"I'm up for it too! Thanks so much, Angel."

I was still anxious when I pulled my car up behind hers on the hill where the parents parked for school. But when we both hopped out to greet each other, I realized I'd seen her once before: at Annie Cusick's pizza party some weeks earlier, where I had mistaken her for a teenager.

Annie and Ian's kids are older than ours—their oldest boy looked to be around eighteen. He was there with some friends on their back lānai, one of whom was with a cute little blonde with a sunny face and a golden, flipped-up beach bob. I'd assumed she was someone's girlfriend. When I explained all this to Angel, she laughed and told me the boy she was with was her oldest son.

As we sat back in her car, she revealed to me the previous week had really been tough; she had just taken that son, the oldest of her three, to the mainland to settle him into college. "I'm really feelin' the pain right about now," she said, her voice soft and clear. She had the faintest Southern lilt at the end of her sentences. Her eyes were a deep, dark brown, mostly bright and happy, but every once in a while the slightest wisp of pain would wash across them. I figured it was because she'd just said goodbye to her boy, but something else seemed to pull at Angel—a yearning to run somewhere far away. Perhaps I was misreading things, because just a fraction of a moment after I'd catch that look, she'd be all sincere sunshine again.

The drive took about fifteen minutes, the first moments of which were awkward, just as I'd predicted. The friction of my Lycra workout pants against her car seat seemed to squeak at full volume with every little shift I made. I tried to fill in the silences with "umms" and "yeahs" and secretly hated myself for being nervous and having no cover. I'd never been able to be cool. But we were more engaged in conversation than not, and at least I wasn't shaking.

We headed out of town along the Pali Freeway and exited in the middle of the jungle at Nu'uanu Pali Drive. Angel explained to me that our destination, the Jackass Ginger Pool, was a natural watering hole complete with a small waterfall and a rock waterslide. She wasn't sure how the pool got its name. I'd later find out it was named after a donkey that, years ago, was tied up near the pool, surrounded by ginger plants.

The beginning of the hike was tricky. We teetered across a wide stream on some slippery, unstable rocks. Once we traversed the stream, though, the hike became an easy walk through a dense bamboo forest. The thick bamboo stalks— the exact green of Kermit the Frog—crossed each other in slashes at the top of the canopy, just below where the leaves started to grow. The crisscrossing of hundreds of stalks at every angle reminded me of modern wallpaper. As we walked, Angel began to explain her past to me.

She had met her husband, Mike, in high school, and they'd married young—*so* young, she said with a laugh, they had to coerce someone to go out and buy them beer on their honeymoon night. Mike joined the navy and served on sea commands for fourteen consecutive years, which meant he was gone on a submarine for six to eight months every year. As a nuclear engineer he served on nuclear-powered submarines, one of which was a tiny deep submersible that only had four beds—called racks—but eight men. They would rotate sleep schedules so that the racks were always occupied and were called "hot racks." He never told Angel exactly how deep the sub could go. "If I tell you, I'd have to kill you," he would say.

On postings that weren't in good school districts, Angel would homeschool their three boys. Although she didn't really complain, I got the feeling she'd had some tough early years and that, in Hawaii, she'd found both a home she loved and a lifestyle that gave her time to spread her wings and explore. Though she'd been on O'ahu for years now, she still held on to a genuine sense of wonder at the extreme beauty all around her.

As we walked, we found a rhythm. That, coupled with the act of looking down while hiking—lest I trip on a huge tree root and fall over the edge of a cliff—made conversation very comfortable. Our back-and-forth was simple and straightforward; I felt I could listen to Angel for hours. She spoke a little more about her older boy having left for college and her realization that all her children would be gone soon, and how even though she was still quite young, a future without them was daunting. I wondered whether she was in the same head-space as mine. Had she lost a part of herself, like me, when she became a mom?

Perhaps that flash of sadness I'd seen on Angel's face meant she was coming to some kind of understanding about exactly how much she had lost and how it would become even more clear once her boys were gone. I waited for her to open up more, but instead she trailed off right at that point of her story.

Perhaps I was projecting my problems onto her.

As Angel stopped talking, I looked up and gasped. We had entered a pine forest—Norfolk Pines as far as the eye could see. The pines were evenly spread and fully grown, the forest expansive. We were no longer in the jungle of Oʻahu, but in England, in Sherwood Forest. The landscape was jarringly, incongruently beautiful. Captain Cook's crew had planted the trees when they first occupied the islands in the eighteenth century, Angel explained, so they'd have wood for their ship repairs. In school, I'd learned all about Captain Cook and his discovery of Australia. He eventually met his death in the Hawaiian Islands, killed by the locals.

At the base of these pines grew the most superbly bouncy, fluorescent green moss beds, like magical fairy mattresses. I imagined hundreds and thousands of tiny winged creatures flying into the forest after dark, dancing around and chattering with each other. After a while they would tire, and they'd flap their transparent wings while descending to the moss like hummingbirds. Then they'd curl up together and sleep soundly in the warm Hawaiian breeze.

I couldn't wait to bring the boys back and show them.

"How have you been settling in?" Angel asked kindly.

I thought about giving her the regular answer: "Great" or "Fine, thanks." But instead I told her the truth—that it had been a complicated start, and I was in a complicated place. I told her about the turn my life had taken in the past several years, how I'd been in a surprisingly long mourning period over the loss of my career and the feeling of failure for never having reached the dreamy heights I'd imagined for myself. I spoke of the strong pull motherhood had on me and how my heartfelt choice—between full-time motherhood and my acting career—was basically the less painful of two painful options.

Angel listened and said very little.

Oh, she's really going to be over this kind of indulgent Hollywood thinking, I thought. *Am I boring her? Or embarrassing her?*

But every time I checked in, I could feel Angel was right there with me, as open, accepting, and clear as the truth I sought for myself.

So I went on to tell her about the fight with Dad, moment by moment—how I had been struggling to bury my lifelong desires of becoming meaningful to the outside world, how the fight had revealed that I'd disappointed my dad and that in failing him, I'd failed myself. Nestor was the only other person who knew about that night, and I hadn't even given him this much detail.

As I relayed the events of that night, the tangled lump of despair I'd been left with seemed to unravel. With every step Angel and I took along the jungle path, I was reaching a new level of clarity.

The ground then became very mushy, and all at once

everything smelled like mulled wine. We had entered a strawberry guava grove and were walking on rotted fruit. The fragrance was overwhelming but not offensive, more exotic and fertile—sexy, even. I looked up, trying to spot the fruit in the trees above.

"I don't know," I said, desperately holding back tears. After knowing Angel for less than an hour, I'd just dumped the totality of my struggle on her. I sure as hell wasn't going to force her to deal with my weeping and wailing. "I'm just very, very lost right now."

Angel nodded knowingly.

By now we could hear the rushing of the waterfall right below us. We clambered down the small descent and reached our destination.

The Jackass Ginger Pool was a perfectly round watering hole with smooth black rock and fallen tree branches two-thirds of the way around. To our right was a small section of lush green tropical ferns. At the back end of the pool sat the perfectly manicured yard of a house on Nu'uanu Pali Drive. The house was rustic, and its lawn was cut short and pristinely, with a row of six evenly placed coconut trees and a tiny entrance leading to the watering hole. The unblemished lawn and orderly landscaping made the pool look like an oasis.

Angel and I sat drinking our water together, not saying much. It had suddenly become easy to let the silence just be. Taking the short route back to Angel's car, we allowed the conversation to lean toward religion and politics—the two most taboo topics among even friends and relatives, let alone virtual strangers on their first meeting. Yet we were able to discuss them with ease.

"Do you have a little more time?" Angel asked when we reached the end of our journey. "I want to show you something."

We got back in her car and drove about a minute up the road, back toward the Pali. Angel pulled off to the side, parking on a narrow sliver of dirt at the edge of the thick jungle.

I squeezed out of the passenger door and followed her to an unmarked opening—the mouth of another trail through another dense bamboo forest. This trail was narrow and dark; at one point, we had to climb over a huge dead tree trunk blocking the path. I didn't ask any questions. Traversing this passage to whatever was at the other side required trust and a little determination.

As had been the pattern of the day, the path opened onto another magical piece of the earth: a large clearing in a narrow gully made by the freeway, which cut through the Ko'olau Range. A rock pathway led to the ruins of an old palace surrounded by soft green grass. Only a few stone walls remained, one quite crumbled and the other still standing, with the doorframes intact. A small plaque explained: These were the remains of King Kamehameha III's summer palace, a modest home he'd built for his Queen Kalama in 1845. Many traditional Hawaiian feasts had been held there, with music and hula dancing and a *kālua* pig cooked in an underground oven. In 1847 it was the site of the biggest lū'au on record, attended by ten thousand people.

Beyond the ruins was a huge clearing that had been made for that long-ago lū'au; it was still very bare. "This is why I wanted to bring you here," Angel said, leading me to the clearing. "Just stand facing the mountains and feel what happens."

I did as Angel instructed, and we stood for a few minutes. Everything was still and silent except for the occasional *whoosh* in the distance from cars on the freeway.

Then it happened.

I saw the wind before I felt it. It came in from the mountains. The sparse leaves on the scattered trees ahead began to ripple, and the ripple moved closer and closer until the wind washed over us like the soft water of a moving sprinkler. If it weren't so breathtakingly warm and comforting, it would have been creepy.

On the tropical island in the *LOST* world, when leaves ripple on trees in front of the characters, a freakishly out-of-place creature like a polar bear or an invisible "smoke monster" is about to run them down. This was not that. This wind soothed me like a shower before bedtime, leaving me relaxed and open at my core. I suddenly felt present, pained by heartbreaking loss but also full with love. Somehow both truths brought me comfort, even as I prayed for courage.

"That happens every few minutes." Angel grinned. "Kinda makes you feel better, huh?"

Trying again not to weep like a big baby, I agreed.

⚜

I am not, by nature, a creature of habit or routine. As my days in Hawaii began feeling more and more like adventures, however, journaling each night was becoming a ritual. I needed to remember the important moments happening almost daily on the island and to take stock of the memories those moments inspired. Writing had helped me remember Prayer Hill and the incredible meaning that tiny piece of road had held for me as a kid. Now I was journaling so I wouldn't forget.

Earlier that day, had I stood on another piece of sanctified earth? Angel hadn't said anything about any kind of spiritual enlightenment, but instead had just waited for the wind to wash over us. She just let me experience it, and that was that. I loved her for letting it sit in me and on me, quietly and peacefully.

After the hike, I felt something shift. It wasn't as though I was suddenly found. I was still somewhat lost and searching for a way out. But now I felt like Dorothy or Alice, lost in a specific, wondrous place—in Oz or Wonderland.

I thought about the character John Locke yet again, and his connection with the *LOST* island. Immediately upon arriving, he experiences the island's healing powers. He feels that, at its heart, the island holds something beautiful. Time—six whole seasons—would prove his theory right or wrong. But on the day of my hike with Angel, I too had felt something transformative in the land. Something had anchored me to it and reminded me to have the courage to look for that connection again.

The thought of beginning such a search gave me hope. I was so pleased about the recent chain of events. My shaking hadn't returned for a while. I had met Patty at Longs, and something emanating from her had encouraged me to come out of hiding. As a consequence, I'd said yes to the hike. And because I did, I found some peace in the Hawaiian earth.

Best of all, I was led there by an angel.

Chapter Eleven

OCTOBER 2009

'd made some friends during our three months in Hawaii, but I was reluctant to think of them as kindred spirits. I was already in danger of becoming a professional friend, and that was not the way to solve my problem of feeling lost.

My cup was already running over with kindred spirits when I'd arrived on O'ahu, and I wasn't looking for more. In fact, I'd been expecting an entirely different search. I had it in my mind that my year in Hawaii would be more solitary. I'd meet new friends, yes. But deep connections would take too much time away from the business at hand: to rediscover my usefulness in the world outside of my children.

The concept of being a "professional friend" was something I frequently thought about. I'd first heard the term nine years earlier while working on a TV show that was shot outside of Hollywood. My castmate Vinnie and his wife, Di (a close friend of mine long before the series began) had just had a baby boy, and she had left her teaching job to be a full-time mom. As with Nestor and our move to Hawaii, the whole cast had relocated for convenience, and Di was making friends with other moms in our new town.

On set one day, someone asked Vinnie how Di was enjoying motherhood. "Oh, she's a great mom," he replied with a smile, "*and* she's a professional friend now."

Vinnie was being funny, but I took his comment seriously. I had no children at the time, and I had an excellent job with good pay. If part of motherhood was becoming a professional friend-maker, then it didn't seem like much of a job at all—at least not an important one. Plus, I already had friends—good friends, in deep and long-lasting friendships. And I thought that when I became a mom someday, of course I'd still be a working actress.

"Love and work . . . work and love, that's all there is," claimed the great psychoanalyst Sigmund Freud. "Love and work are the cornerstones to our humanness." Freud was of great use in theater school, especially when it came to understanding the writing and thought processes of leading modern realist playwrights like Anton Chekhov. In Chekhov's plays, especially *Three Sisters*, the characters who don't work moan about needing to do something, and the ones with no love lament about being alone. The very few people who work *and* have love are the ones with the greatest shot at happiness. Yet I had always seen love and work as two completely separate entities, and my mindset hadn't really changed since I'd become a full-time mom.

Throughout my life, I had been blessed in the kindred

spirit department. I was hitting the thirty-seven-year mark with Jenny and Katrina, who grew up around the corner from me. At age four, we couldn't possibly know what kind of people we'd grow into, but we'd gotten lucky: Our friendships had stuck and grown only stronger and stronger. Then Kerrie had joined our kindred circle in seventh grade, and the four of us stuck close to one another, tending to each other's wounds when we messed up badly or got our heart broken by a boy. We'd become each other's bridesmaids and maids of honor, and we continued to cherish our friendships even after that. And of course, I had Nestor, who is my ultimate kindred spirit—my soul mate.

Despite my hesitation to become a vocational friend of sorts, I had met lots of moms in LA since the kids were born. I had even formed a few strong friendships that had gone past the "mommy playdate" with women I'd met through the boys' school. So I sure didn't need soul mates in Hawaii.

Yet I'd already bonded so easily with Angel on the hike. And then I met Barb, Joey's mom, who—true to her word—set up a playdate with the boys at the Mid-Pacific Country Club, a small, low-key golf club set back in the hills of Lanikai. A hidden gem with million-dollar views of Lanikai Beach and the Ko'olau mountains, the club had an outdoor restaurant and a pool for the boys to swim in. And Barb was the perfect hostess.

It was a nice relief from some of the first-time playdates I'd happened upon in Hollywood, where I'd be the only mom surrounded by non-English-speaking nannies when the other moms failed to explain they wouldn't be there. Or I'd end up alone, a free babysitter for all the kids, while the other mom took the time to run errands and get things done. But Barb was eager to hang out with me and another friend, Rikke, who had a son in the same grade. Barb asked me a ton of questions, and if ever the conversation drifted to a topic unfamiliar to me, she and Rikke were careful to fill me in on the backstory. The conversation flowed easily between all three of us, and Rikke, an incredibly kind person, has one of the most fantastic laughs I've ever heard. It starts with a high-pitched "whoa" followed by a "ho, ho, ho, ho, ho," with each "ho" quickly descending about a half note. It's hard not to laugh along with her.

Barb reminded me of Di: just as interesting when talking about her day-to-day existence with her kids as when she was opining about a big life issue or event. I could tell she liked to be in the here and now with her children. That was certainly my goal, once I could rid my head of all the doubts. Barb was energetic, quick to laugh, and interested in every minute detail of what Rikke and I said. It was as though she had nothing else on her mind.

But we were talking around the elephant in the room. No one mentioned Barb's husband in Afghanistan, and I certainly felt it wasn't my place. Finally, the right subject came up: Barb explained she had met Joe in college in the South and then moved around with him while he was training with the army as a surgeon.

Rikke put her hand on Barb's arm and asked how she was doing.

Barb allowed Rikke's hand to stay there for a while. "I'm good," she replied at last. Then she looked at me. "This is Joe's first deployment. The army has given us so much. They subsidized Joe's whole medical education, and it was really time for us to give back." Her diction sounded elevated, like a politician's wife giving a well-rehearsed speech.

She looked down then, and I realized she was gathering her next thoughts, arranging her concluding sentence. "I just hope and feel that because they've invested so much in his schooling, they'll take good care of him."

Barb paused for a moment. Looking flushed and warm, she moved her hands up to her thick blond hair and shook it, fanning the moisture off the back of her long neck. Then she looked me solidly in the eye. "I don't know," she said. "I'm scared. I'm trying to train my mind not to go there."

And *boom!* Just like that, her cover was gone. She never tried to put it back on. She let herself become the vessel of her undisguised truth—completely direct and heartbreakingly vulnerable. I had the urge to hug her like I used to hug my girlfriends in Australia when they were sobbing with a broken heart. By letting me in to what she was feeling, Barb had taken me home.

As Barb continued to talk, she pulled out of her bag what looked like a long silver chopstick. She twisted her hair into a flawless chignon and then jammed the stick through the middle at just the right angle to keep it all perfectly in place.

"Wow, that was impressive," I remarked.

"Oh yeah, that's my thing," Barb laughed. She explained that after her friends had kids, they all found something they were good at. "All except me. Jocelyn used to be a professional ballerina, and now she's taken up photography. Jess has started a jewelry line, and Lili is the Hawaii state manager for Miller Coors. Everyone else had something special they could do, and I was just a housewife!"

I laughed upon hearing this, but really it was as if she had blown one of those whistles only dogs could hear . . . and I was the dog.

"But then Jocelyn said, 'No, you can do that amazing thing where you put your hair up with a stick. That's special!'" Barb continued. "So that's my thing."

You feel it too, I thought. *The Freud thing. Love and work . . . work and love. That's all there is.* Barb's eyes held the same sad look I'd seen flash in and out of Angel's eyes as she wondered what the next step would be after her boys went to college. Love and work . . . What would *she* do next? We were all feeling it.

And I loved Barb instantly for saying it out loud.

As Rafa and Joey's friendship grew, so did mine and Barb's. She introduced me to her close circle of friends, who are as easygoing, kind, and straightforward as she is.

Halloween rolled around, and Irene and Scot—whom I'd met through Barb—called to invite us to their annual trick-or-treat party. Scot was a marine. Irene had once described his job to me by saying, "You remember Kelly McGillis in Top Gun? That's what Scot does! He's Kelly McGillis!" They lived on the north side of Kailua, in a part of town called Kaimalino, right by Marine Corps Base Hawaii. Kaimalino—meaning "calm sea" or "peaceful sea"—is a small enclave where the streets are flat and quiet and filled with homes from the 1960s and '70s. It could've been the Brady Bunch neighborhood, but for the

hundreds of palm trees, the soft sea breeze, and the thick layer
of stars that glistened in the night sky.

On the night of the party, Barb showed up a little late.
"I've just been FaceTiming with Joe," she said with a nudge as
she sidled up next to me.

I always felt better whenever Barb arrived at a party. She
was like my license to be there. Having her around made me
feel a bit more secure—my buddy by the bean dip.

"How is he?" I asked.

"He's doing great," she answered cheerfully, but she looked
a little dismayed. "He says he loves us and misses us, but he's
in a . . . a zone."

"A zone?" I asked.

Barb nodded. "He assures me the kids and I are the most
important part of his life. But there's nowhere on earth he'd
rather be right now. He even loves the food." She looked at
me quizzically. "Who goes to Afghanistan right now and says
they love the food?"

"I guess that's . . . good?" I said, knowing I was simplify-
ing things. Barb was relieved and happy every time she spoke
with Joe and learned he was good—and more importantly
alive. She was perplexed by how well he'd taken to life at war,
although her eyes were smiling and I could see she was in love
with her husband's quirks. I sensed Joe was perhaps as complicated as Barb was straightforward.

Once darkness fell, it was time to head out. Irene and
Scot had loaded a big red wagon with ice and many different
adult cocktails as well as water bottles for the kids. Irene took
great effort to remember the water. The previous year, Scot

explained, there had been nothing suitable for the children to drink, forcing them to suck on ice cubes.

There were sixty-one of us trekking around the neighborhood together—thirty kids and thirty-one adults—all in costume. The kids' pumpkin-shaped candy buckets were illuminated with glow sticks—a mass of glimmering, bobbing orange balls of light floating down the street. The sky was a deep, dark grey, lightly smudged by some dour, lingering clouds. The moon hung low and loosely, as though it might fall out of the sky at any moment and smash into a million golden pieces. Staring up, I noticed it was wearing a distinct jack-o'-lantern face. The eyes, the triangular nose, the messy mouth—I could see it clear as day.

I gasped and pointed it out to Nestor and Lili, another new friend. "Go and have another piña colada!" they laughed. But the moon *did* have a Halloween head.

Then Barb came up beside me. "I see it, Shannon. It really does look like a carved pumpkin," she said with a thrill in her voice.

I looked at her, all dressed up in her grandmother's vintage Lilly Pulitzer dress and a shiny aqua bead necklace, her pale hair in a small beehive with wispy pieces blowing across her face. She was keeping it joyful at Halloween for her kids—and for her and Joe's friends—while he worked tirelessly putting back together the bodies of young soldiers. She was running fast, really fast, to keep up, filling in her days as much as she could and trying to stay brave. Yet she stopped and saw that Halloween head in the moon, and she was as happy about it as I was. There was no getting out of this one—I was looking at a kindred spirit.

That night as I wrote in my diary, I marveled at the fact

that I'd stumbled on this group of women so easily and they'd embraced me so willingly. I thought about Angel, too.

Is it the island that draws the warmth out of the people here? I wrote. Maybe the steady heat weighs down their bones a bit, expanding their muscles and flesh so their hearts are more open and available. *Or perhaps the island isn't drawing those qualities out of the people, but instead drawing that kind of person to it.*

My questioning had led me once more into *LOST* territory. In the last seasons of the show, viewers learned that forces on the island had caused the plane to crash and brought the survivors there for a reason. The accident was no accident. Was life imitating art here in Hawaii? Perhaps the island was drawing me to it . . .

We *had* thought about having Nestor commute to Hawaii as in previous years, but instead we'd decided to relocate. I began to realize this was no coincidence. Living on the island and experiencing its beauty day by day was not only making me feel good but also—like on the day of my hike with Angel—starting to heal me. And not only were the people I was connecting with in such a profound way giving my family and me great comfort and pleasure. Their friendship was also teaching me something: My work as a full-time mom was a labor of love. I was working to take care of the little people I loved the most.

But was it enough? I wasn't sure of that yet.

Love and work . . . work and love . . .

I *did* feel sure about one thing: A key component of my work as a mom was having other moms around me doing the exact same work.

Were we professional friends? We were a support group for sure. We were a crowdsourcing system that provided group fun for the kids and an opportunity for them to develop their social skills. We also proved that for us moms, there was strength in numbers. We preserved each other's sanity by together conquering our shared dilemma of full-time motherhood and isolation. We were a think tank, with no "mom problem" too trivial for us to collectively address and resolve. And we were a babysitting service, always willing to watch one another's kids when necessary.

I had a group of friends like that in LA, but I hadn't really seen the value of it until I'd stepped back and found it again in Hawaii. One of the best parts of mothering is to have your friends around you, laboring at their loves, too. I'm not sure that I was their professional friend or they were mine. But I am sure we were each other's blessings.

As I pondered these questions, an image started to come to me: a long line of my friends kneeling by a river, with our babies on our backs, chatting and washing our clothes under the warm sun. Di was there. Barb was there. My best friends from Australia were there with their kids too, whom I had loved even before I set eyes on them. My friends with no children were also part of this scene, enjoying the light, ready to hold a baby at any time.

My river was beautiful and winding, and it flowed steadily with an abundance of water. It was strong enough to be reliable but not overwhelming. And I was so incredibly grateful. And in the reflection from the river I saw an important part of me that had been made good and whole, solely through the love of my friends.

What a gift, I thought. *What a gift.*

Chapter Twelve

NOVEMBER 2009

Carved pumpkins don't last long in the tropics. We had placed ours on two pillars at the beginning of our driveway, at the entrance from the street. After being up there only a day or two, they'd already looked deflated and worn out. By the morning after Halloween, they were completely black with mold, collapsing in on themselves like a balloon that had lost its helium, signaling the party was over.

The moldy jack-o'-lanterns also felt like a little sign from God, as though He were shaking His finger at me from upstairs, telling me, *Halloween is over! Time to go to Mass and forget the fun.*

I wasn't ready to listen, however. Not yet. I wanted to keep the fun going. It felt important to me—emblematic of my new feelings of hope.

We'd been going to Mass on Sundays, not because we were

stellar Catholics but because Rafa was at the age to make the sacrament of the Eucharist—his First Holy Communion. So we'd signed him up for preparation classes at Saint Anthony of Padua in Kailua, and part of the deal was that when Rafa took the 10 a.m. class, we'd go to the 10 a.m. Mass, followed by a half-hour class for parents. We soon discovered one and a half hours of church was too much for a four-year-old, so I usually stayed home with Marco while Nestor attended the service.

On that first morning of November, I wanted to break routine—to have us all skip church and go to the North Shore together. I'd been talking to Nestor and the boys about trying out a bike path I'd spied a few weeks earlier while driving past Sunset Beach and Banzai Pipeline, two big-wave beaches that are flat as a lake in summer. I'd been keeping up with my bike riding around Kailua, and even though it was exercise, the landscape had been a constant feast of visual delights. The bike path I'd seen up north looked less expansive and more rustic. I was eager to explore.

"Let's just skip one day," I begged Nestor. The drive up to the North Shore can be long if you hit traffic, and a late start could ruin the whole day. "One day won't hurt. Mass is so dreary! Come on—let's have some fun."

"We had fun last night," replied Nestor, who is far less apt to break the rules than I am.

"Let's have more fun," I whined. "Let's have an adventure!"

He reluctantly agreed and went out to load up our bikes on the minivan.

The boys were in their usual Sunday morning spots watching cartoons when I shared the news with them. Their Halloween candy was spread out on the coffee table, their booty already counted: Rafa had sixty-two pieces, while Marco had forty-seven. They were super excited about skipping Mass—and nonplussed about a day of biking at the North Shore.

The traffic wasn't bad at all along the Kamehameha Highway up to Sunset Beach, but finding a place to park was exceptionally difficult. We finally wedged the minivan into one of those "almost" parking spots at the edge of Sunset. As we were lugging our bikes off the rack, Nestor checked the tires one by one and decided they needed more air. The back ends of the bikes stuck out into one lane of the highway, and cars were swerving and honking, but Nestor was oblivious.

This is one of Nestor's "husband habits" that drive me crazy. Like many exceptionally bright people, he can lack common sense.

Why is he so impractical sometimes? I fumed.

I just couldn't understand why he hadn't done all his safety checks in the calm of our garage. In fact, I questioned why he was doing them at all. He was more likely to be run over by a car right then and there than to have an accident because of low tire pressure. So I nagged at him to stop.

This, of course, is one of my "*wife* habits" that drive him crazy.

He ignored me, which pissed me off, so I nagged him some more. As he ignored me even more resolutely, the boys looked on wearily. Part of my mind wondered whether I was making it harder or easier on their future wives. Either way, our fun Sunday was suddenly not so fun.

Once we'd gotten on our bikes and made our way to the beach, we discovered the reason for the heavy traffic: a big professional surfing contest taking place on Sunset Beach.

Surfing!

My spirits were immediately buoyed again.

I grew up on Sydney beaches, watching boys who would become some of the best surfers in the world. The four of us sat on the sand, watched the competition for a while, and then began our ride.

The path was as beautiful as I'd expected it to be. At times we'd ride beside the front yards of colorful beach houses with stacks of sandy boards, rusted bike racks, and old skateboards scattered all about. The faint smell of coconut surfboard wax fell in and out of the breeze, occasionally overpowered by the strong scent of the plumerias. A little farther along, we found ourselves on a stretch that was completely canopied with wildflowers, which seemed to grow more abundantly on that side of the island, with more purples and pinks.

We crossed a few old wooden bridges, and it felt as though we were on a country path in the south of France. And then as we left the canopy . . . *bam!* Instant blue as a tropical North Shore beach slammed into view. There was no mistaking where we were. It was all good.

Marco still had training wheels on his bike, which made him slower. We had decided to take turns riding ahead with Rafa, then circling back to switch off and accompany Marco. His plastic training wheels against the concrete path created a loud scratching sound; we could hear him before we could see him. Once I was at his side, he beamed up at me and shouted through the din, "My bike is so loud, isn't it, Mommy?"

Marco, we were quickly discovering, was his father's child: His head was in the clouds, daydreaming about this or that. He'd be easily distracted by a lizard or a bird and ride straight off the path or into a person or a bush. I'd have to help him up, brush him off, and apologize to whomever he'd run over, while asking if their shins or their toes were okay, before placing him back on his bike and getting him moving again. It was slow going.

After some time—too long, it felt to me—Nestor and Rafa rode back toward us and announced they'd reached the end of the trail at a snorkeling beach called Shark's Cove. We decided to turn around and head back.

"No!" screamed Marco. "I want to ride to Shark's Cove too!" When we explained it was a long distance away, and he'd be really tired from the ride, he became unusually still. A steely defiance set into his little face.

This threw us all. Marco had always had a very happy nature. Nestor's dad—or "Abu," as the kids call him—loves to give people nicknames. When Marco was a year old, Abu was spending significant time with him and started to call him "Always Smiling." The name stuck. Right now, the cold look on his face was unusual—and a little bit scary. All three of us were quick to give in to his demand, riding the painstakingly slow journey with him to Shark's Cove and the even slower one back to Sunset Beach.

We rested on the sand and watched some more of the surfing competition until it was time to ride back to the car. Marco complained a bit about putting his helmet back on, and then acquiesced. As we rode down the path, however, something was missing: the grating noise of Marco's extra wheels. When I looked back, he was still sitting on his bike but frozen in place. He hadn't moved an inch.

"C'mon, Marco, let's go," I beckoned. People had begun

packing up and leaving the beach; tons of cars were pulling out of their parking spaces. But there sat Marco, very small in the distance now, with a kind of murderous resignation emanating from his dark features.

We all called for him to move. Nothing.

We rode a fair way forward, hoping Marco would follow. Nothing.

"Come on," I shouted. "Ride!"

He just sat there, refusing to budge. The usual twinkle in his eyes had vanished, and instead they were burning black with anger.

Nestor and Rafa got frustrated with Marco's antics and rode on ahead, leaving me alone to tame the monster. "Wait, you guys!" I called to them, but they pretended not to hear me.

Unbelievable, I thought, sighing deeply with dismay. And then something hit my chest with an invisible thud. I felt pulled back from my expectations of a carefree adventurous morning and pulled into another life, a life of duty—my pedestrian life. My life of motherhood.

I went straight into my yoga breathing, trying in vain to control my urge to let loose an unbridled, uninhibited, four-year-old temper tantrum of my own.

"Move, Marco. Move!" I yelled. "MOVE NOW!" I'm not sure yoga breathing has ever really worked for me.

Marco did not move an inch.

"All right, I'm really leaving," I barked, turning around to pull a lame mom move—the faux exit—even though I knew he was too savvy to take the bait.

The sun had come out from behind a cloud, and the direct heat on my head was starting to simmer my grey matter, making it hard to find a solution that wouldn't involve me losing my cool among the crowd. I began to hate Marco. I started to resent him even more as it dawned on me he had probably set it up this way. That's why he was as cool as a mob boss.

So I pedaled back to my savvy antagonist, got up close in his ear, and hissed, "If you don't move your bike right now, I'm going to give you a very big punishment."

He continued to stare me down.

"All right," I whispered, "if you don't follow me by the count of five, I'm going to"—I had to think quickly—"take away all of your Halloween candy."

Shoot, I thought immediately. *That punishment is too big.*

He and Rafa were both so proud of their Halloween stash. Marco had been careful to only eat one piece so far. But the threat was out there, and I had to follow through. After all, we were now at DEFCON 2.

As I slowly pedaled away, I counted out loud—"One . . . two . . . three . . . four . . . !"—all the while desperately thinking to myself, *Get on, you little shit. Please get on.* "Five."

Marco didn't move a muscle.

Oh no.

I couldn't believe the Halloween candy threat hadn't worked.

He looked like a miniscule Tony Soprano, his black eyes fixed on me, his tiny milk gut hanging from beneath his shirt.

That was it.

I threw my bike down and thundered toward him.

This must have startled him, because his bike slipped from his hands and fell over the curb, into the back of a parking space—just as an old van full of surfboards was preparing to pull out.

Marco squatted down to retrieve his bike, and suddenly he was wedged between the van and the curb. Smoke was coming out of the van's exhaust pipe, and I could see that if the driver slipped into reverse, Marco would be squashed.

"MARCO!" I screamed so loudly I startled even myself. "GET UP NOW!"

Then it hit me: This was my fault, because I had ignored my duty.

Marco had displayed some defiant behavior at school a few weeks earlier, and I'd basically ignored it. Rafa was settling in, which had been a great relief to Nestor and me. I was on a nice run too, making friends with some great women and connecting with the land; my anxiety was easing too, as I healed from the argument with Dad.

We'd noticed slamming doors and other loud noises were startling Marco, and he seemed a little dazed sometimes, but he was still amiable and sweet—although not so much on the day his teacher had pulled me aside.

Before the final cleanup of the school day, she told me, Marco had lain across a table and refused to budge. The kids were forced to clean up around him. Was he upset? Was he just tired? The teacher couldn't get it out of him.

He was normally an obedient boy, especially in school. The problem was that Marco was our baby, and Nestor and I found everything about him exceedingly cute. The image of him sprawled obstinately across the table was just funny to me; when I told Nestor, he found it funny too. I knew the teacher didn't find it funny or cute. Marco was not her baby, and she had fourteen other kids to deal with. When we'd questioned him about it at home, he'd given us nothing, so we dropped it.

But there had been more.

Just a few days before Halloween, the teacher pulled me aside at pickup time again and gravely explained Marco had been in trouble that day for calling two little girls "pieces of poop in his pocket."

Where does he come up with this stuff? I wondered. I had trouble containing my church giggles and looked tentatively toward his teacher to see if she might commiserate with me in my guilty amusement.

The teacher didn't crack a smile. The two girls were able to swing higher on the swing set than he could, she continued, and he wasn't happy about it, so he began his verbal attack.

I pulled myself together and assured her I'd get on top of the situation.

I had been meaning to pull Marco aside and work on this. He was acting out about something, and I needed to find out what it was. I was the one who knew him best. He was at the age when his speech was a little garbled, and at times I was the only one who could understand him.

I needed to break this wild horse of his defiance. He had to respect his elders. He needed boundaries and rules. He needed people in authority to like him—people outside his family, people who didn't think he was adorable like we did. But I hadn't wanted to do that mom work just then, although that work would make his life easier and better for him in the future. Instead, I'd wanted to have fun, to escape into this new life I was falling in love with. Love means hope, and I'd been too busy hoping I had started to heal.

So I ignored my duty. I ignored my son. And Marco was done with having his problem ignored.

🧠

Back at Sunset Beach, I had a dark flash that I was going to lose this tiny person whom I hated in that moment yet loved even more than life itself. But the van rolled forward, and Marco jumped up and away from it.

I grabbed hold of his arm. "What are you doing?" I yelped. "That truck could've crushed you! What were you thinking, Marco?"

By this point, a small crowd had gathered, but I was too incensed to look around me—although I did notice two big local guys standing next to where the van had pulled out. Actually, I'd been ogling them before we'd even gotten on our bikes that morning. Both were handsome and shirtless, with huge muscular biceps and intricate Polynesian body art displayed up and down their shiny arms. They looked like brothers or cousins—sexy brothers or cousins. But to a four-year-old whose eye level most likely hit their kneecaps, they probably looked intimidating. That gave me a wonderful, awful idea.

I walked up to Marco, held his little face between my hands in a firm grip, and spoke very clearly and directly in his ear. "Get on that bike right now," I ordered him calmly. "And if you don't pedal and come with me, I'm going to leave you here, and one of these big Hawaiian guys is going to take you home to live with him instead."

I was not proud of my words, but at last Marco jumped on his bike. And boy, did he ride! He rode so fast that by the time I retrieved my own bike, I had trouble keeping up with him.

As we approached the minivan, I passed a few tanned, sandy girls with gorgeous bodies in bikinis, tiny babies slung casually on their hips. *You won't be so chill in a few years,* I thought bitterly. And I tried very hard not to cry as I trailed Marco to the car.

Marco was in big trouble. Rafa was so mortified to hear his brother would be losing all of his Halloween candy that *he* started to cry. No tears from Marco, though. He just sat there. Guilty. Resigned to his fate and perhaps to his darker nature. And just like that, my fairy-tale run of love and hope had been flipped on its side.

But Marco didn't ruin my "happily ever after," and the moldy pumpkin was not a warning sign from my fairy god-mother to monitor my intake of fun. My darkness was real, and it lay inside me, entwined in my ambivalence about the life choices I'd made and my continuing inability to sit peacefully with those choices. As I realized this, a fury grew in me, as though I were a bank robber whose lucky spree had been cut short. I was caught and caged, and forced to take off my mask for all to see the real me.

As we drove home on the Kamehameha Highway, I stared out at the Pacific for a long while. I thought about Marco at the Halloween party the night before, dressed as a little banana— how he'd looked so small and a bit lost, trailing behind all the other kids. Even though everyone was enamored with him, patting him on the head and calling him "Banana," he'd struggled to keep up. I'd noticed all this, but now I couldn't remember if I'd gone to him and helped him at all. I'd been caught up in the magic, too busy loving the fun to look out for my son. Why had I done that to him?

Maybe I wasn't cut out to be a mom.

Finally, I spoke softly to Nestor about my doubts regarding the severity of Marco's punishment. Nestor assured me I'd done the right thing. We had to "rein Marco in." He needed to learn the consequences of his behavior were real, to respect authority and the boundaries we were laying out for him. This would only benefit him in the long run.

We drove on, and moments after making this proclamation, Nestor started to mouth his lines for the next episode of *LOST*—quietly, but loud enough for me to hear. And I began to hate him even more than I'd hated Marco on the bike path.

SHANNON KENNY WILL BE A
FAMOUS ACTRESS

Motherhood is a selfless job, and actresses by nature are not selfless people. The ocean looked so clear and close I had an urge to jump from the car and swim away—partly to escape, partly to hide my shame. Then my emotions, as mercurial as that ocean, flipped and I was angry again. This time my anger turned toward all the people in Hollywood who didn't hire me, who prevented me from fulfilling my true calling.

You motherfuckers with power, screamed a voice inside me, crying out to all those nameless suits who had said NO. *Why didn't you like me? What was it I lacked? What made me not good enough for you?*

I had worked so hard. I had trained to be a good actress so I could elevate their crappy material. I could have made their words sing and their stories fly. I worked so hard. I was built for that life! And yet here I was, in a whole different reality.

I should not be your victim! A woman does not go to motherfucking Hollywood to become a wife and mother!

SHANNON KENNY WILL BE A
FAMOUS ACTRESS

I was desperate to get out to that ocean now, to put my head under and into the cool and get away from all my doubts and the chump in my head who cried, *Victim!* I had to get away from my family—to swim without stopping, without coming up for air.

Hadn't I made any progress at all over the past weeks? One bad moment, one mistake, and the ground had become shaky again. I was dismayed, but also frightened at my yearning to flee.

True to the fluctuating nature of my feelings, I changed course again and landed back on earth. I knew that regardless of the urge, I'd never do it—I couldn't leave the boys or Nestor willingly.

But I also knew they deserved so much better. They deserved a mom who was at peace with being a mom, who wanted to sit in the muck and glory with them, without all the self-obsessed, big life questions swirling around in her brain.

And they certainly deserved a mom who didn't ask questions of faceless executives who didn't know, remember, or care about her.

Did the boys pick up on my despair? Was that why Marco was being so defiant? It didn't matter—they were stuck with me.

I was so tired all of a sudden.

I put my hand back to rub their sandy feet, which were dangling from their car seats. I caressed Rafa's foot and then Marco's, and was surprised when he didn't flinch. As I soothed him—and myself—I made a wish on his foot, rubbing as though it were a magic lamp. I wished for clarity and peace of mind as I determined to do better from that moment on, to be one thing and one thing only: the best mom I could be.

Chapter Thirteen

DECEMBER 2009

"**S**ee how crowded the beach is?" I said to Nestor and the boys as we found a small place on the sand to lay our towels. I pointed out the surfers who were already competing in the water. The crowd held their collective breath every time someone rode through a barrel wave, disappeared inside the foam, and then came flying out the other side still standing, pumping a fist or flipping the shaka—the "hang loose" symbol, which is a sign of reverence or respect in Hawaii. "This is Hawaii's favorite sport," I declared gleefully.

We'd almost reached the halfway mark of our time on O'ahu. Our weekends were precious, but I had developed an obsession—a need to visit the North Shore beaches and catch as many surfing competitions as I could. The contest we had stumbled upon the day of the Marco meltdown had whetted my appetite, and since then I had made the pilgrimage as often as I could.

In the beginning, I rationalized my renewed interest as resembling the renewed passion some golfing fans had after Tiger Woods hit the scene. Surfing is the sport of Hawaii, and it's only natural I had become a fan. But it's also a big sport in Australia, so it made a certain kind of sense. I had gone full circle in wanting to be part of that world again.

Back in November, I had talked the boys into going with me to see the first final of the Vans Triple Crown, the start of an important three-part contest. To eventually be crowned the Triple Crown winner is a huge honor in the surfing world—the equivalent of winning the Kentucky Derby—and it was taking place in our backyard.

We can't miss this opportunity! At least that was my pitch to the boys. I must have sounded convincing, because they'd accompanied me quite willingly to the first final at Haleiwa Beach.

Nestor was working, so it was just the three of us. Once we arrived, I was thrilled to point out a plaque with engraved names of previous winners, dating back to 1983 (the year of its inception)—including one name that belonged to a classmate of mine from high school, plus a few other names of guys I'd hung around with as a teenager.

Then I saw an older surfer who was making a comeback, preparing for his heat. "I used to know him," I said excitedly to the boys. "He would come out to Avalon Beach in our winters, when the waves were smaller here in Hawaii. He sort of hung with the crowd I was in." I was exaggerating. I didn't know him. I just hung out with a crowd that milled around him, but it was more impressive to the boys if I stretched the relationship a touch.

I used to know a lot of surfers, but this guy was particularly wild. I remembered him going to jail at one point, though I didn't mention that to the boys. Besides, they were there for the surfing. I could've talked to them for hours about my old life, but they weren't really interested.

I could remember, with a strange lucidity, every detail of those couple of years I'd spent as a surfer girl, from tenth grade until about a year after high school graduation. Somehow, that time was much clearer in my mind than so many other parts of my life, as though I'd lived it in Technicolor while other years had played out in splotched and muted tones like a damaged movie reel. As we navigated our way across the busy beach, I began to wonder why.

Our time was limited, owing to their short attention spans, but the surfing and atmosphere were great. I tried to get the boys into the showman aspect of "riding the tube," but that held their interest for only a little while. It took a lot of concentration for them to focus on the small figures surfing the break far out at sea. Marco wanted to play on the shore, which was tricky because there were a ton of photographers, videographers, and watercraft all over the place. It was tough for him to understand that the beach, usually a child's playground, had now been converted into a sports arena for adults.

I found myself mesmerized by the groups of boys and girls in their late teens sitting together, enjoying the surfing but enjoying each other even more. Golden surfer girls in bikinis were a pleasant distraction for the young men with salty, sun-parched hair, who probably were dying to get out there, catch some waves, and strut their stuff. I watched them laughing and tormenting each other, shifting constantly to different towels, playing games by pretending to study the surfers as they ignored the person who wanted their attention. Light drama was playing out, but there was no worry on their faces. They seemed to delight in their games of cat and mouse.

I remembered that age and gazed at them with a deep longing to be there again.

In Australia, I lived in a small village called Mona Vale—a beach town that sits along a narrow peninsula whose tip juts out into the Tasman Sea in the South Pacific Ocean. Just a few towns north is Avalon Beach, the beach where we all hung out—our teenage meeting and mating ground. I usually rode the bus to get there, along a winding road we called the Bends, atop a cliff overlooking another beach called Bilgola.

Once you're out of the Bends, which extends from the north and south headlands of Bilgola, and you begin your final descent into the town of Avalon, there is a tiny stretch where you can see the waves of Avalon Beach. When I'd look at the variegated blue and white curling water, a thrill would rush over me.

It would be Saturday, in the late afternoon—the school week over, and my homework done. All that would lie ahead of me was the beach, my friends, and the feeling of possibility—the possibility that after tonight, a shift might happen inside of me. The shift would alter nothing, really, except the way I saw my life.

The shift was love.

Maybe I'd fall in love with someone. Maybe that someone would love me back. And then my life would look beautiful.

Because I longed for that change, my arrival in Avalon would fill me with anticipation. The shift was possible. It could happen that very night. I knew it was possible because it had happened once, right there on Avalon sand.

Kerrie and I had been at a party in Avalon, in the back-yard of a small beach bungalow, when she spotted a boy she thought was cute. He was sitting down, leaning against the back fence. As we ambled by, the boy called her over. I remember being impressed with how fast my shy friend had gotten the job done—she must've been making eyes at him.

Being a good wing woman, I sat down on the scratchy grass, next to the guy's friend, who also sat with his back against the fence. He had one leg outstretched and the other up while he rested his elbow on his knee. I saw him quickly drop a ciga-rette and stamp it out with his shoe as he saw us approach. He was pale with ashy blond hair, shaved at the sides and full on top. He had a slight overbite and a lazy eye, which made me a little unsure of where he was actually looking. He wasn't hand-some, but his face was interesting, and he looked intelligent. His name was Paul, and he sat there watching another boy who was drunk, thrashing around on the grass. Kind of disturbed by the kid, I brought my knees in close to me, wrapping my arms around them for protection and pulling down my skirt.

Paul cringed as the drunken boy bumped into people, caus-ing them to spill their drinks and back away to give him space. "That's my cousin," he said. "He's more like my brother, though." He went on to explain that his mum's sister had abandoned his cousin when he was a baby, and he'd lived with them ever since. Then he told me his dad had recently died of cancer, and he felt sorry for his mum, having to raise two boys on her own. We watched his cousin in silence.

Then Paul and I started talking. We talked for a long time because Kerrie and her guy would not stop chatting. When we finally left, she told me the two boys were going to take us out to the movies in Avalon the following weekend. I didn't really want to go. Paul was nice and funny in a wry sort of way, but he wasn't handsome or breezy—not at all like someone I'd fantasized about.

I agreed to the plan for Kerrie's sake, and the big date arrived. After the movie (*The Best Little Whorehouse in Texas*), the four of us decided to head across the road to the beach.

Instead of exiting up the theater aisle, all three of them bounded over the seats. I tried to do the same, but my jeans were too tight, causing me to become wedged between two headrests. Luckily, the boys had hurtled ahead, and Kerrie was the only witness to my clumsy recovery and walk of embarrassment up the aisle with the other uncool people. Once we hit the sand, we separated. I knew Kerrie was eager to fulfill *her* fantasy, which was to kiss her boy . . . a lot. Instead of walking far, Paul and I sat straight down on the sand under the lights of the surf club. I asked him some more about his dad, and about how his mum and cousin were doing. I liked hearing him talk about this awful time in his life—not out of morbid curiosity, but because it *meant* something.

At a slight pause in the conversation, as I was digging my fingers into the sand, Paul slowly put his arm around my shoulder. I wasn't expecting it. I looked up from the four perfect finger holes I'd made, and he moved his face close to mine and kissed me, slowly and with purpose.

My stomach fell away. I lost my breath and my chest ached. I had never felt anything as good as him in my life. It was shocking. I spilled into him, and I felt beautiful. We kissed and kissed and kissed.

Going home on the bus, Kerrie told me that kissing her guy made her want to vomit. She was completely over him now, and he gave her the creeps. Then, she laughed nonstop when she remembered me getting stuck between the movie seats. But I had shifted on the inside. My lens had changed, and everything looked golden. When I thought about Paul, it hurt to breathe. All I wanted was to be beside him again and look at him and talk to him and kiss him some more. My whole life was suddenly different. I had kissed guys before, but that night I learned what a kiss could really mean. I'd discovered romantic love, and for the next few years that was all I wanted.

My schoolwork still mattered. I still wanted to be an actress. My family and girlfriends were strong, meaningful connections in my life. But now my teenage body and mind were mostly governed by a deep yearning to love and be loved in a romantic way. I had that with Paul for a short time, and then I lost it. I was devastated. I searched for it again and found flirtations here and there, along with one big, true love. Then I left Avalon for America and left those surfer-girl years behind me.

Now here I was in Hawaii, trying to recapture that thrill. It was December, and I was determined to see the second final of the Triple Crown—and this time, Nestor joined the boys and me back at Sunset Beach, on the North Shore. As the final surfers took to the waves, Rafa enjoyed imparting to Nestor a little of what I'd taught him about the sport at Haleiwa a few months earlier.

"That's a barrel wave, Dad," he crowed. "You get extra points for that."

Once again, as at Haleiwa, I found myself watching teenagers sitting on the sand in lovely ignorance, skipping from moment to moment with no clue that the world might have any kind of gravity in store for them. The silliness and laughter, even the heartbreak and tears of that time, came rushing back to me, but I couldn't recall ever worrying or ruminating at that age—only fantasizing.

I fantasized almost as much as I lived. I fantasized while listening to boring school lessons or waiting for the bus, while scooping ice cream at my afternoon job, while drifting off to sleep. Fantasizing is so different from contemplating or second-guessing; it propels you forward into a world you yearn to inhabit. In a typical fantasy, I'd be lying on warm sand, close to a faceless boy. And when he'd tuck a piece of my hair behind my ear, that warm rush of love would run through my body.

As I looked around me now at the young faces on Sunset Beach, I realized something: My trips to the North Shore had me fantasizing too, only I was now being sucked backward as I fantasized about the past.

The Triple Crown had drawn me in. I wasn't just into the surfing competition; I was into the world it transported me back to. Traveling up to the North Shore allowed me to relive those few short, vivid years before I came to America.

Well, this is a bit depressing, I thought. *If I'm coming up here because I miss being in the first throes of young love, does some insane part of me think I can find that again?*

I wasn't about to do something stupid. I had a few friends whose marriages and families had fallen apart because someone yearned uncontrollably for that youthful feeling. Nestor and I had been together sixteen years. We'd had our honeymoon years a long time ago. Finding that feeling of new love would require . . . well, a new love. But I still wanted Nestor.

At least I could figure that part out. So why did I feel so empty, so suddenly old?

Wriggling beside me on the sand, Rafa was still sharing his newfound wisdom. "Dad, look! He's a surfer from the olden days. He's a friend of Mom's."

Nestor looked at me and raised one eyebrow.

When the day was over, I could see it was a one-time thing for Nestor. He'd seen a surfing competition, and it had been fun, but he didn't really need to do it again. While driving home, I decided I was done too. I'd just been yearning for a lens change, a beauty rush. The North Shore had reminded me of a short era in my life, when new love hit me hard and propelled me through time on a sweet, hot breeze that made me forget everything else on my mind.

But a few weeks later, I drove up to the third final, at Pipeline—alone this time. "I just have to go," I insisted to Nestor. I had to see the Triple Crown through to the end.

As the first glimpse of Sunset Beach came into view, I

suddenly felt the rush of possibility—that same thrill the teenage me felt as the bus rounded the Bilgola Bends and entered Avalon.

I drove a little farther on to Pipeline and parked, then walked to the beach and sat by myself on the crowded sand. I looked around hopefully, trying to catch the vibe. And I saw it. I recognized it. But it only really appeared in my periphery. I couldn't *feel* it. Everybody else was with friends. It was an unusual place to be alone. My being there felt premeditated, superficial, and strange, as though I were trying to squeeze myself into the pages of a small book.

Those years I was yearning for had been short. I left for America right in the middle of the best of those days. I left a group of people I had *belonged* to, at a time when there was still so much possibility. My best Aussie girlfriends stayed in that beach crowd much longer than I did. I still sometimes ask them about someone we knew back then, and I'm sure they sense the nostalgia in my voice.

"Ugh, why do you want to know how *he* is?" they answer. "He's so gross now. Why did we ever think he was hot?" They saw everyone grow old, but I never did. In my mind, those people will always be stuck at a beautiful age, forever young and reckless and magnificent. Those were the days when fun and our love of one another were the most important things of all. I have never, at any other time, felt so free.

As I gazed out at the Banzai Pipeline surf, three thousand miles away and twenty-three years later, the penny dropped. There was a reason I felt so free during those years: I had abandoned a great deal of my ambition to be an actress. My changing body and its teenage chemistry demanded I satisfy my need for love as a young woman, and *that* became the overriding force I lived by. Back then, in many ways, I was closer to myself than I'd ever been, either before or since . . .

Huh, I thought, staring into the blue Pacific, the other side of the same ocean I grew up on.

Then it *truly* dawned on me: That shift I sought back then, that desire for love and possibility—I had already found it. Despite my acting goals, which made me leave everything, travel across the world, and face my life alone . . . and despite the jobs lost and won, the constant fight to keep going, to stay sane and happy, to finally accept failure . . . despite all of that, somehow I'd managed to reach my unfettered surfer-girl goal. I had found love—real love, true love. Love I didn't ever want to leave or lose. And I was loved—now threefold.

I paused for a minute, alone on that crowded beach, and a part of me came back from somewhere deep inside. I loved that part of me, that surfer girl. I picked her up and slowly packed my things, then walked her back to the car and sat with her for a while. Then I started the engine and drove with her, away from the North Shore and toward our windward side of the island. An hour later, I arrived at our house, where the family I love was waiting for me.

I love, and I am loved. That girl and what she wanted, I have. We've reached our goal, our pure surfer-girl goal—the goal that was everything.

Chapter Fourteen

JANUARY 2010

I am no lover of exercise. I rode my bike in Hawaii for one simple reason: to lose weight. I was still trying to shed the pounds I'd gained from my pregnancy with Rafa and then Marco on top of that.

I have always struggled with being disciplined about exercise. Yet somehow I became a consistent rider in Hawaii, and it was the landscape that kept me coming back for more. On those rides, I experienced moments of visual magnificence, moments of intense and profound beauty that put me in a state of almost incomprehensible awe—until I started to make sense of it all by way of God.

I was a sincere Catholic when I was younger. I talked to God often, as though he were an invisible friend but older, like a grandpa. I kept absolutely nothing from him; anything on my mind was fair game. I figured if he was all-knowing, he knew everything about me anyway. Many years later, however, my communication with God had faded to almost nothing—until I started riding my bike around Kailua, when I found myself talking with him again.

It was often the middle of the day when I went out on my ride, while the kids were at school. My usual path took me south along Kalaheo and up the hill toward Lanikai, then down around the back of the Lanikai Loop on Aalapapa Drive, ending in a climb up the hill again to the Lanikai headland. Getting up the hill was taxing, so I always paused at the top to sip some water and turn my gaze eastward, toward the beaches. The colors of the sea were always different shades of blue lined up like a Rothko painting or a more orderly Van Gogh sky. The water was mostly clear, and every time, without fail, I yearned to immerse myself in it—to become a physical part of the living art.

One day in January, time got away from me, so Nestor watched the boys while I rode out later than usual—a little before sundown. I reached the Lanikai headland on my way home, just as the sun was setting behind the Ko'olaus to the west, drawing my eye in the opposite direction—away from the ocean. I'd never been there at that time before. Pink and orange beams that were flecked with tiny golden halos radiated through the narrow gaps in the mountains and pointed up into the sky like a heavenly laser show. I was literally seeing the view in a whole new light.

Whoa, I thought, balancing on my bike and watching the sun set. *This is more than art. This is God.*

My heart rate dropped, to the point that I wasn't exercising anymore, as I just sat and stared.

That was amazing, I said to God silently. *Thanks for letting me be a part of that.*

❀

Ever since I'd quit acting, I'd been down on the floor and God had been up somewhere very high, out of sight and beyond feeling. I'd been pleading with him to fill the hole in my chest, to help me not be so lost anymore. But while I'd been begging him for help, I hadn't thanked him for any blessings. Now, after that first sunset ride, I started talking to God like I did when I was young, as though he were right beside me and all around me.

Rafa began asking to join me on my bike rides. At first I was hesitant, unsure of whether he'd be able to navigate the traffic on the sections that are open road. But there was something about that amazing sunset that turned me around. And so I allowed him to come—and I was happy I did.

On Rafa's first few rides, I was on his case, nagging him about watching for cars in all possible directions. He was patient with me and took on the responsibility with focus and pride. We often paused at the top of the Lanikai headland to enjoy the view—whales out to sea and many more heavenly sunsets behind the Koʻolau mountains.

One day, coming down the hill on the backside of the Lanikai Loop, with no need to pedal, we rested our hands on the brakes. I was in front, with Rafa close behind. All of a sudden, a large ibis flew in between us. It seemed to glide on the small jet stream I'd made with the speed of my bike. The ibis was big and quiet and coasted between us longer than a wild bird should. We were silent, hoping it would stay with us as long as possible, but once we reached the flat road, it flew away.

"Oh my gosh, Mom, did you see that?" I heard Rafa call from behind. "Did you see that?"

"I saw, Rafa!" I answered.

"That was the most amazing thing EVER," he cried out.

Once again I thought, *That was from God—or from someone who had been with God.* Had a person, a soul, been sent down to us—someone who had been in our lives at one time? Even though I've never really had an existential crisis, never questioned my faith that God existed, the reminder was gold. It was reassuring and calming and monumental. I said another silent *Thank you* and again felt him beside me, no longer out of reach.

The gifts just kept on coming.

Another time, I was riding along Mokulua Drive, the beach road that runs parallel to Lanikai, when I saw a young guy coming off one of the many beach paths, carrying his kayak and paddle. He was shirtless, muscular, and tanned. I slowed a little as I neared him. He loaded his gear onto the back of a pickup truck and then lifted a huge water-cooler-sized jug up and over his head. This was not a jug you buy at the store, but one of those you have delivered—like a small barrel. As I rode closer and slowed down even more, I noticed his biceps flexed from the weight of the container, and I could see the slender veins in his forearms bulging beneath his bronzed skin.

Oh no, he isn't, I thought excitedly. And then I *really, really* slowed down, until I arrived at the best seat in the house. *Oh no, he isn't going to . . .*

But he did.

He poured the water all over his body, and while I stared in awe at the refracted sunlight bouncing off the crevices of his eight-pack and glistening all around him like a hot halo, it seemed that time had stopped for a few seconds.

Holy moly, what a beautiful sight.

When this magnificent outdoor shower was all over, I caught my breath and thanked God for about the hundredth time that month. Back at home that day, I wrote about it in my journal. Then I turned on the television, and the news streamed in: A massive earthquake had just hit Haiti.

This was *the* Haiti earthquake—and as I watched all the early footage they later deemed too distressing for audiences to view, the death toll continued to tick up to over one hundred thousand. The clips were horrifying: people wandering aimlessly around the wreckage with their hands on their heads or shaking them in the air; young mothers holding babies, covered in dust, with pain etched on their faces; dead bodies pulled out of chalky, crumbling walls that had been too flimsy to withstand the earth's power. One woman ran down the street wearing nothing but shorts, her sagging breasts bouncing as she screamed, "The world is coming to an end!"

If I were there, I'd have agreed with her. It looked like Hell.

I glanced away, out the window toward our lovely beach and the ocean shining with its usual splendor. Here, God seemed to be shining his light everywhere.

Why not there? I asked myself.

The newscaster shook his head and said, as if replying directly to me, "It is just . . . There are no words."

But I knew I'd have to find words this time. I'd been

spending too much time with God to have no answer. Rafa had been attending Holy Communion classes for several months, and he was old enough now to wonder why such a tragedy happened. It was our job to guide him, to tell him whether God had a reason or had simply made a mistake—or if he had any control over Mother Nature at all. And given the utter devastation in Haiti, I'd have to confess whether I still believed, unquestionably, in God at all.

❀

The earthquake in Haiti was the kind of world event that puts everything into perspective: the value of human life, the need for people to help one another, the inequity that exists between the first and third worlds. Mother Nature is as beautiful as she is cruel, and life is limited. Death not only is sad but can be ugly, torturous, and incredibly unfair. My worries about being lost instantly faded as I began to search for ways our family could help the people of Haiti.

A few days after the earthquake, Nestor and I awoke to find the boys had made a care package. While watching cartoons, they'd seen a commercial calling for aid in Haiti. They'd found one of our moving boxes in the garage and filled it with cans of food as well as blankets and decorative pillows (that belonged to our rental house owners). As if to underscore their innocence, they then asked for help with the address and stamps.

They were so savvy with technology, so skilled with language and already so worldly (having come from a huge metropolis), it was easy to forget they were just babies and all heart. We explained that, for the time being, it would be best to send money, which would get there faster. They had a small chunk saved: Marco gave two dollars. Rafa gave twenty. Nestor and I donated as well. We called the number on the TV and pledged our money, right then and there.

I was feeling pretty good about our efforts until I dropped the boys off at school the next day and saw a banner for a stuffed animal toy drive. One genius young student had come up with the idea: ask kids to buy a small stuffie with their own money and bring it to school so he could collect them and send them to a Haitian orphanage. That afternoon, I picked the boys up from school and explained the concept as I drove them to the toy store. They were very happy to pick out the toys, and as we reached the cash register, I was thinking that despite dropping the ball in so many ways, we had still managed to raise the kindest, most empathetic kids I knew—aside from the superhero kid who'd come up with the idea in the first place.

As the salesclerk rang up the purchase, I handed each boy an envelope containing the remainder of his savings. Rafa was aghast. He'd thought *I* was going to pay for the stuffies.

"Jeez!" he cried and threw up his hands. "I've already given them twenty bucks. I mean, can't they buy their own stuffed animal?"

I pulled him away from the register and explained that Haitian children lived in one of the poorest countries in the world to begin with, and now many of them had lost their toys, their home, and their town. There was nowhere for them even to *buy* a stuffie. I debated telling him the children had also lost their parents, but decided to keep quiet on that front.

Rafa, giving me the death stare, reluctantly handed over his money. If he'd been bald and wearing glasses, he would have looked like a pint-sized Larry David. After I recovered from my mortification, I realized Rafa's behavior made complete sense for a seven-year-old. He had already made his sacrifice for good, and now he was done. It was an unacceptable but understandable—and totally human—perspective.

A mere three days after the earthquake had struck, amid massive outbreaks of cholera and more deaths, my empathy had also waned as I became inured to all the dreadful images. Mostly what remained was the Big Question: *Why? Why did God allow this to happen?* I'd managed to morph Haiti's real, deathly, destructive third-world catastrophe into a first-world, self-involved, existential crisis in my head.

As so often happened that year, *LOST* was there with an answer.

There was an exchange in the show I couldn't get out of my head. It was between John Locke and the show's hero/antihero Jack Shephard. It happens in a moment where the survivors are looking to Jack to lead them off the island. Jack is reluctant to do so, and John Locke agrees with him by saying he'll never be able to lead until he himself finds out where he is going. The island needed some of its mysteries solved before the survivors could escape, and solving those mysteries required faith in the mystical world. Jack, who had declared himself a man of science from the beginning, struggled to accept certain things he'd seen and heard on the island—events that proved the island held inexplicable powers. As Jack started to question the foundation of his beliefs, he became unsteady and ambivalent about leading.

Like Jack, I didn't know where I was going. How could I lead my children when some of the biggest questions—about my life and about life in general—continued to confound me?

Of course, I knew *some* things.

I knew being good was hard work. I also knew—from my acting days, ironically—that human nature has a great capacity for good but also for bad. I'd gained that knowledge from studying so many characters and taking note of so many people. Gathering insight had been a part of my job.

All the great plays were written with characters whose nature comprises both light and dark. Moral ambiguity is the norm. While working on scenes from *Macbeth*, I'd learned that the easiest access into Lady Macbeth, who murders and cheats through the whole play, is her love for her husband. She is evil in action but sound in motivation.

Shakespeare was a master at bringing these kinds of people to life: Hamlet, Richard III, Othello, Shylock—all are recognizably human because of the duality that sits in their souls. And, of course, in life there are human monsters: despots, terrorists, child predators, racists, sex traffickers, serial killers. I was pretty sure my kids would not fall into these categories. Still, I had work to do every single day to steer them toward their better selves. How was I going to help my boys with that work?

Jack couldn't lead until he figured out where he was going.

I had no idea where I was going, but Rafa's behavior in the toy store and my short attention span for Haiti made it clear: I needed to find out. Soon.

✿

Despite some moments of resolve, I found myself muddling aimlessly through those days in January, with no idea where to start the work. Out of necessity, I continued with my perfunctory duties: making breakfast, dropping the boys off at school, shopping for food, picking the boys up, overseeing their homework, squeezing in some fun, making dinner. And then, for half an hour at the end of the day, right after the kids had eaten and before their bedtime, I'd duck out for a walk on the beach while they watched *Phineas and Ferb*. Our time in Hawaii was coming to a close, and I wanted to take advantage of my days by the ocean.

I'd always walk in the same direction: north. First, I'd walk straight down to the shore, digging my toes into the top, wet layer of warm sand that had been heated all day by the sun. Then I'd wait for a small, cool wave of water to wash over my feet, and stay still as the sand melted away. This was my very own end-of-the-day foot spa. Kailua is on the eastern side of the island, and the moon dictates most of the light at that time of day, so the beach is often soaked in grey and blue tones. Sometimes, a small glow from the last bit of sun behind the Koʻolaus creates a silver sheen that makes the white water glisten like snow.

It would take me exactly fifteen minutes to lay hands on the volcanic rock at the end of the beach—the barrier of Kailua's northern crescent. After touching the wall, it would take me another fifteen minutes to walk back. But for no particular reason, a few days after the toy store incident, I decided to walk in the opposite direction, toward Lanikai. It was a much longer walk to the south headland of Kailua, so my plan was to time myself fifteen minutes one way and then turn around to head home.

On my way out, I ducked under so many fishing lines that when it was time to head back, I decided to walk on the top end of the beach, away from the water. Looking up at the row of beachfront houses, I saw something I'd never noticed before: a church steeple, behind the houses, lit with that faint residue of sunlight from the mountains.

Where is this beautiful church? I wondered, until I realized it was *our* church, Saint Anthony of Padua. A chill went through me. This was a sign.

It crossed my mind that perhaps I was too caught up, once again, in the world of *LOST*, where signs were implanted in every episode—numbers, mythical figures, statues, names and literary references—to guide the survivors to their destinations and give them clues about the island and its purpose. But for me, this steeple *was* a sign—a good sign, the right sign, and perhaps the answer to my questions about leadership and God.

The sign pointed me toward our church.

Rafa was still preparing for Holy Communion, but I had continued skipping Mass and the half-hour class for parents after Mass, using Marco as an excuse to stay at home instead. I was the bad Catholic. Nestor had been going as our representative, leading our family forward. He knew it was important to be in the class for Rafa's sake.

Joey was studying for his First Communion too, so Barb had been begging me to go to church. She was nervous the other parents in the parish would think that with Joe gone, she had taken up with Nestor, as they were the only two singles in the parent class. I'd teased her about it, and although she laughed, I could see the tiniest part of her was worried about the rumor mill. Barb was so good! She had her hands full with a younger child but still went to every Mass and every class. She'd even converted to Catholicism when she married Joe.

Thinking about all this, I knew I could do better for myself and my family.

Standing on the beach and staring at the steeple, I realized I wanted to be like Nestor and Barb. I might not have known exactly where I was going, but it seemed clear my next step should be to go back to Mass more willingly and regularly. I did believe in God, and I had faith. I'd simply forgotten to practice it.

Faith, by itself, had become flimsy and faded for me. I needed to nurture it through ritual, through learning and working at it. I thought of my friends whose marriages had dissolved in part because they allowed too much slack in their connection with their partner. While they were dealing with life's other stuff, they had let the rope between them loosen, so much that it fell out of their hands. I feared the same thing had happened with my relationship with God.

But now that steeple was pointing me in what felt like the right direction. Going back to an actual brick-and-mortar place of worship was a tangible solution that might give me clarity and purpose. I'd grown up going to Mass, so it was the natural place for me to return. And so I did—we all did.

The next Sunday after Mass, Nestor, Marco, and I went to

the First Communion class. I sat next to Barb, and she patted me on the knee.

"I'm so happy you're here," she said, beaming. "It's really boring, though."

She was right—the class *was* boring. The Catholic Mass could also be pretty dry and challenging at times, especially since my beliefs don't always jive with the orders trickling down from the Vatican. But the Mass is always good of intention, always built around the objective of helping humans act in accordance with our better selves. It's beneficial to be reminded of that—week in and week out.

There are pastors and nuns around the world who adopt disabled children as babies and raise them with care and love until they die—at which time their hearts break for the babies who had become true sons and daughters to them. These stories abound in the church, and every week at Saint Anthony's we prayed for one of these people. It helped to have a goal like that in mind—a person who could be a true inspiration.

At almost every Mass, I'd remember a line from one of the testaments, or recognize a truism from the homily, or catch a special look between two family members in a pew, and it would stick with me through the rest of the week. Those small moments fueled my quest for answers about the bigger issues in life. Mass became another guaranteed place to talk to God.

Rafa *did* eventually ask me the Big Question I'd been waiting for, though in a more myopic way than I'd expected. I'd been anticipating: "Mom, if God is all good and all-powerful, then why does he let bad things happen in the world, like the earthquake in Haiti, where all of those little children were killed?"

Instead I got: "Mom, if God is only meant to do good things, then why does he let bad things happen to us, like the teachers giving us homework every day?"

I had been thinking for some time about the answer to the Big Question, so I jumped in on it. "Well, here's what I think, Rafa," I began, explaining that perhaps God is not meant to do only good things and that maybe he wants us to have struggle in our lives. "Without bad things, we'd have no appreciation of good. "Christmas Day every day would feel pretty ordinary after a while, right? Too many treats wouldn't taste so delicious because you'd be feeling sick. Too many toys would feel over-whelming, and the meaning of Christmas would be lost. We need other days to contrast with Christmas—regular work-filled days, perhaps hard days—so there is a little bit of dark to show us the beauty of the light."

In order to do this, I explained, God had to give up some of his power. He had to give us free will. This means there is some room in our minds to do bad things as well as good. So sometimes people choose to hurt each other—they choose their darker nature, their "mean selves," as I told Rafa.

"I think he left room for darkness in everything he created, and that means Mother Nature, too," I continued. My think-ing is that he didn't make her completely perfect and good, which is why bad things can happen with the earth that God can't control. Some people think differently, but that is what I came to believe in that time.

"Although I'm not sure homework qualifies as a bad thing," I said to Rafa, "even though it might feel like that. But ultimately it may make you smarter and give you good work habits, which is a *good* thing. A *bad* thing would be like the earthquake in Haiti, where not much good comes out of it at all, and there is destruction and innocent people die."

I explained that after these things happen, God needs us to help one another and do good things and be more loving than ever. He needs us to bring out our light side.

"God needs *our* help. That's one of the reasons we've been going back to Mass—because we need to keep practicing doing good and being kindhearted. I like to think we are helping God just like he is helping us. Do you get it?"

"Yeah," Rafa answered, and then he asked me, "How do they get those traffic lights to sit on the pole with just those two grey bolts?"

I'd lost him. But I'd figured it out for myself in some way.

Maybe God needed *me* a little when he led me to that sunset and the magnificent young man on the beach. Maybe he needed me to see that steeple, the same way he brought that beautiful ibis to Rafa and me on our bike ride. Maybe he was sending out signs all over the place, for *anyone* who would see them.

My theory is that God had known a big earthquake would hit Haiti. He knew that a really big, bad, tragic, and unexplainably sad event was about to happen and that many souls would perish all at once. It would be a lot for people to handle. People's belief in him would be shaken and tested. I think he was terrified. I think he needed the faithful to stick by him. God needed us.

Perhaps I was right; perhaps I was wrong. Free will means just that: freedom to believe what your own reason and your heart tell you. I believe I owe him my faith and my assurance, especially after all the good things he has given me. And it seemed right to teach my kids to do the same.

Ultimately, as is the way with God, he gave back even more. My renewed faith meant I now had a better sense of self, which made the hole in my chest smaller. And because he needed me, I felt of service to him somehow, which gave me extra purpose. That lifted some of the weight from my "lost" pile, and carrying a lighter burden made me feel more found.

Chapter Fifteen

JANUARY 2010

If you are the type of person who stays with a TV show until the very last credits roll off the screen, you might have caught a glimpse of a unique love affair—a beautiful relationship that carried through all six years of the *LOST* series. Unlike onscreen romances, this was one love story the audience was never privy to, yet it was revealed in a single sentence at the end of the credits:

THE PRODUCERS GRATEFULLY ACKNOWLEDGE
THE COOPERATION OF THE PEOPLE OF HAWAII
AND THEIR ALOHA SPIRIT.

Perhaps this statement was shown for a legal intendment or a political reason of some sort. It is true the people of Hawaii possess a welcoming, benevolent, easygoing vibe—an "Aloha spirit." I also learned that underlying this spirit is a complicated history and an understandable resentment of the European settlers who colonized the islands—one that runs as deep as the molten rock beneath this paradise.

Ultimately, we weren't in Hawaii long enough to glean a firsthand understanding of it all. But when our family arrived on Oʻahu as part of the *LOST* production, we were welcomed with open arms. From where I stood, as a close observer with an inside pass for that final year of the series, the love affair was real.

At no time during our year in Hawaii was that passion more evident to me than on January 30, at the show's biggest celebration: the *LOST* season premiere in Waikiki. It was the night of the Sunset on the Beach event, the night I let Nestor down by hiding in the security tent to avoid walking alongside him on the red carpet—the night my failure felt so overwhelming I wanted to be erased from my own life.

The funny thing is, I had been really looking forward to that night. Meeting Nestor's fans is fun. He is never stingy with his soul, not to anyone. It always feels like a little happy dust is sprinkled around us for a moment. People imagine our lives to be fabulous, and it's nice pretending that it's true.

The cast and crew of *LOST* were always treated with kindness by the people of Oʻahu—a kindness that sometimes morphed into reverence for the actors. On the whole, the actors returned the love; most of them were on the ride of their life thanks to the show's success and the joy that came with Hawaii living. Some families were flat-out refusing to leave Oʻahu after the show was over. They had become active members in different community groups, and their kids were settled and doing well in school. This was the best place many of them had ever lived. Only scoring another regular acting job would make it worth relocating.

As time went on, it became clear Hawaii not only welcomed the *LOST* family but celebrated us. Strangers would recognize Nestor in the grocery store and stop to tell us stories about a friend or relative who'd worked on *LOST* as an extra or a crew-member. Everyone seemed to love the show, taking ownership and pride in it. That supernatural world was like their own little kingdom, and Nestor—and the boys and I, by virtue of relation—were living in the kingdom's castle.

We even wondered whether the boys were benefiting in school from being kids of an actor on *LOST*. Rafa seemed to make friends more seamlessly than he had in his first year of elementary school in Los Angeles, where every other child was an actor's kid too.

I, of course, felt great living in the metaphorical castle after spending my whole life trying to secure a spot up there. I never felt superior when meeting *LOST* fans—I was a *LOST* fan myself, after all—but the attention made me feel noticed, and that felt good. I was happy being caught up in Nestor's recognition even though I'd never reached the level of stardom he had attained—happy to be seen beside him, just because I loved him. So my actions at Sunset on the Beach made me question whether I'd made any progress at all in my quest to be at one with myself again.

Organized by the town of Waikiki and paid for by the city of Honolulu, Sunset on the Beach is a regular event with a thirty-foot screen erected at Queens Beach in Waikiki, so locals and tourists can sit and watch a movie in the open air, just on the heels of the setting of Waikiki's brightest star. With the pink-and-orange-sherbet sun fizzing away slowly in the ocean, it's easy to see why the sunset is as big a draw as the movie. But Sunset on the Beach turns into a huge event when *LOST* airs its first episode of every season on that enormous screen.

Throughout the island, the night swells into an epic celebration of all things *LOST*. Producers and other actors and just about everyone told us this was *the* event to look forward to. They described the long red carpet and thousands of fans standing behind barricades, cheering like they were in the midst of Beatlemania. The actors and their partners would walk a press line before being ushered to front-row seats to view the episode. Afterward, we'd attend a fancy party.

I had bought a nice bottle of champagne and chilled it in the fridge all week so Nestor and I could enjoy it on our limo ride into Waikiki. I'd put some thought into my outfit, too, opting for jeans and a gauzy blouse with some snazzy gold sequins around the neckline and sleeves. Bohemian chic seemed a perfect way to go for this glamorous event on the beach. But in the final days before the event, I began to feel a massive regret about the way my body looked. It was a problem that weighed heavily on me.

As heavy as a bag of flour.

I hadn't thought much about my weight up until I was twenty-seven and working on my first American TV series, *Muscle*—the show where I met Nestor. I didn't look in a full-length mirror too often, but I'd always liked the way my body looked. Even before moving to Hollywood, I'd been long and lean, benefiting from a high metabolism. Added to that, I was a bundle of nervous energy. As teenagers, Kerrie and I both had restless leg syndrome; when we were together, her dad had to leave the room because our nerves made *him* nervous, and he couldn't take it in stereo.

On *Muscle*, I was cast to play a sexy younger wife who inherits the gym that belonged to her husband, after he catches her making out with his son in the steam room and suffers a fatal heart attack. In that scene, I had a towel wrapped around me, but in most scenes I wore a tasteful business suit with a matching mini skirt, à la Heather Locklear in *Melrose Place*. The dressing room for the costume department was a dingy, fluorescent-lit space on the sound stage that had been thrown together with some cheap plywood walls. That's where all my days of not obsessing over my body came to a startling halt.

I had carefully marked out a little section of floor that was free of stray straight pins, so I could model without injuring my bare feet. Standing in front of a semicircle of mirrors one day, wearing the most sophisticated outfit I'd ever had on my body—a creamy silk shirt that felt like cool liquid on my skin, and a perfectly tailored-to-my-ass-and-thighs pair of silk trousers—I thought I looked fantastic.

As the lead costume designer and I gazed at my image, she nodded her head and said, "Bag of flour."

"I'm sorry?" I asked.

"A bag of flour," she insisted.

I had no idea what she was talking about, so I just stared at her, bewildered, until she clarified: "A bag of flour. That's all you need to lose. Five pounds."

"Oh," I replied, unable to think of anything else to say. I'd always thought I'd looked great in clothes.

I went home to my apartment that night and jumped up and down in the bathroom, trying to get a look at my whole body in the vanity mirror above the sink. I didn't own a full-length mirror. I didn't own a scale. I never wore skintight clothing, and I was rarely at the beach anymore. The only time I was really naked was in the shower.

I looked down at my tummy and saw a teeny-tiny pouch. I pulled at the skin near my hips—there wasn't much to hold on to, but they felt soft and perhaps a little more curved.

The seed of discontent had been planted.

About five years after that, I stopped booking work for a little while, longer than usual. But I was auditioning well, taking class twice a week to stay in shape as an actor, and receiving excellent feedback from my teacher, who was considered one of the best in town. So why wasn't I getting work? I couldn't figure it out.

At home in Australia that Christmas, I was driving in the car with Mum and lamenting over my dry spell when she pulled over into a beach parking lot and turned off the car.

"Shannon," she said to me, "Nestor and I have been talking about which one of us would tell you this. I'd never say this if you were my daughter the teacher, or my daughter the doctor. But you're my daughter the actress, so I have to say it."

"What?" I asked.

"You've put on some weight," she replied. "That might be why you're not booking jobs."

I immediately burst into tears. "I'm fat?" I wailed. Sure, I had noticed my clothes were getting tight, but I had brushed it aside, more concerned that I was doing something wrong with my acting. I could've kicked myself for missing an obvious reason why I hadn't been booking. "Oh no! I've blown everything!"

"Maybe I shouldn't have told you," Mum wept. Her reaction whenever I suffer a big hurt is to join in on the tears. "I just thought it would be for the best."

"Oh God, oh God" was my only response, which made her cry even more.

"I shouldn't have told you," she sobbed.

"No, it's good you told me. I'll be all right," I whimpered. "I'll just have to lose the weight."

"Yes," she said, brightening a little. "You've got my Italian blood. We have curves, and we have to watch what we eat." She suggested I go to Weight Watchers like she did, claiming it was really good and not that hard. "Oh God, I hope I did the right thing by telling you."

The penny dropped. So that was why Nestor had been taking me on so many jogs during that Christmas trip—really hard jogs where I'd curse him under my breath as he'd climb another headland. He was trying to fix my problem his way. At that time I was still very driven to succeed as an actress, so I kept up those jogs until our Christmas vacation was over. Once we were back in LA, I attended Weight Watchers, where I learned I had three bags of flour to lose.

How did I let things get so out of control? I wondered. I felt like an idiot for concentrating so hard on my acting and simply failing to see I'd gained weight.

I shed those fifteen pounds slowly and steadily—and just like magic, I started booking jobs again. Losing the weight was quite uncomplicated. I suppose Hollywood was nothing if not consistent in the way it wanted its women to look, regardless of their acting ability.

Ten years, two children, and six bags of flour later, my weight gain and my drive to fix it were far more complex.

Without the threat of being seen on screen to push me into action, my motivation just seemed to hang in limbo. The discontent I harbored about my weight lingered every day at the periphery of my consciousness. It hurt enough to make me think of it often and to bum me out, but not enough to hold my concern for very long—or to make me eat less and exercise more.

Some of my girlfriends in LA grew up with parents who were critical of their body and their weight. For those friends, I'd noticed, working out and dieting were a top priority. I knew they often had an unhealthy mindset, but at least they stayed in shape. I grew up with a good body image, but my mindset was not particularly healthy either. The way my body looked made me sad, yet I had done little to remedy the problem. And recently, socializing with my new friends had resulted in consuming more calories from eating and drinking than even my regular bike rides could burn off.

On the cusp of the *LOST* premiere, however, reality hit me in the face. That dissatisfaction slid from the periphery and settled into the front and center of my mind. As the day continued, I felt more and more depressed about the weight I had gained since having children, and about my inability to lose such a big chunk of it.

The buildup had been steady and solid since the birth of the boys. By the time of that January 2010 event, that woman who had started to enjoy living up in the *LOST* castle and being seen next to her prince . . . the woman whose husband wanted her there for support as he maneuvered through the push of fans and the press . . . even that girl from just a few years ago, who had craved the spotlight for herself and wanted to be noticed as a princess in her own right . . . had somehow become the kind of person who would choose to be invisible.

⚜

Two days before the *LOST* premiere at Sunset on the Beach, Angel told me Annie Cusick had been juice fasting for days in preparation for her appearance beside Ian on the red carpet.

Oh no, I thought. *I haven't done a thing about my weight.*

So, on the Saturday morning of the big night, I informed Nestor I needed the whole day to myself to prepare. I set off for our small hometown Macy's in Kailua, whose building had been there since 1946 when it had originally opened as a Liberty House department store. My purpose was to buy a back-fat-minimizer bra, and then some new dewy foundation and a pair of false eyelashes. The idea was for the last two items to make my face so glamorous it would distract from what was happening from my neck down.

I moved slowly all day, as though wading through mud— or through my own six bags of soggy fat-flour. I tried on a million bras, which did nothing for my self-esteem. Once I eventually found the perfect back-fat eraser, I lingered in the parking lot on my way over to Longs Drugs just to see if our mystery storefront had a big line outside. It did. I paused in the sun, trying yet again to think of what else the store could be—a ballroom dance club? A trapeze and tightrope training center? No, the building wasn't big or high enough, and neither of those would explain the line.

Then I shook myself out of it and tried to refocus on my mission.

When I arrived home, Nestor was shocked at how long it had taken me to purchase just those three items, and I had no idea where the time had gone either. I only had about an hour to get ready. I needed to wash and dry my hair, shave my legs, apply my makeup and eyelashes, get dressed, figure out the boys' dinner, kiss them goodnight, and then hobble out to the car in my highest heels (which I believed made my legs and butt look thinner). I almost accomplished all the tasks in time, but for the frickin' eyelashes.

I had never put on falsies before. The trade winds were down, which meant the humidity was up and the glue was slimy, not sticky. Because I have small eyes, the lashes looked crooked and strange; they needed to be trimmed. I couldn't find a small pair of scissors, so I was coming at my eyes with huge kitchen scissors.

Time was ticking. I started to sweat, and the back-fat bra started to cut into my back. My fresh new makeup just looked greasy and thick. Worst of all, my eyelids felt as though they were carrying ten-ton weights. I feared that if I blinked too much, my upper and lower lashes would stick to one another. So I stopped blinking, which caused my eyes to water and my liner to run.

When the limo arrived, I still was not ready. Nestor was agitated that I was causing us to run late. "Take the bottle of champagne from the fridge and bring it to the limo," I

shouted. "I'll be there in a second." He came back a few minutes later, bottle in hand. It was a town car, so we were not
legally allowed to drink the champagne.

I began to lose it. Popping the bottle open, I chugged
a few big sips and burped my way out of the house, barely
catching a buzz. That's when I realized I couldn't face the
photographers or the red carpet—no matter how many times
Nestor reassured me I looked beautiful. For him, it was no lie;
he loved me and still found me attractive. But Nestor was just
one person. Inside me still lived the girl who wanted multi-
tudes to adore her.

SHANNON KENNY WILL BE A
FAMOUS ACTRESS

Would I ever be rid of that little girl? The hole in my chest,
which usually felt frigid and vacant, was now an inferno.

❀

At my place in the security tent, exhausted from watching the
swarming crowd and making small talk with the other shy
partners, I felt a tap on my shoulder.

Nestor.

His face was red and his eyes were glazed over, like a president or a senator in a receiving line at a political rally. He
appeared to have checked out, like he'd gone somewhere,
removed himself from his body. It seemed impossible for

anyone to receive that much glorification and still remain humanly present.

"Come with me," Nestor said, leading me to a break in the crowd just before the start of the press line. Standing there, among thousands of people, were two familiar faces: my girl-friends Angel and Jayne. They were holding up two signs:

WE ARE FANS OF SHANNON

WE ARE FANS OF ANNIE

Angel and I had built on our friendship since our first hike to the Jackass Ginger Pool. We sometimes walked Kailua Beach together, and she'd bring along a bag to collect trash. Kailua Beach is quite pristine, so I'd think, *She won't find anything to pick up*. But without fail, Angel would spot a tiny bright blue bit of fishing net or a miniscule piece of plastic and pop them in her bag without skipping a beat.

Through Angel, I had met Jayne—a transplant to Hawaii with her family from New Jersey. In 1993 Jayne survived a deadly mass shooting while she rode a commuter train home from Manhattan. Twenty-five people were shot and six were killed as the shooter fired at people point-blank, making his way from one end of the car to the other. Jayne told me she and others got on their stomachs and crawled the length of the train car to escape the carnage. She quit her job on Wall Street shortly after and became a full-time mom. When I asked her how she coped, she said simply that for years she attended a memorial for the six who perished. I could see that Jayne was living her life like a survivor, making every minute count.

These are two quality women, the best sort of friends, and they were there with a blessing, a gift, a sign—a literal *sign*, for goodness' sake!—intended for me. They had battled traffic, found an impossible-to-find parking spot, and waited in the crowd so they could share that love. Annie had seen it on her way down the red carpet, but Nestor had to pull me out of hiding so I could receive that wonderful gift. Even then, it took me a few days to fully realize what they had done for me.

I might have been slow—I was in my forties and still craving superstardom!—but I was not stupid. I understood what they were giving me with that sign, and I thanked them with all my heart, hoping they had some idea of how deeply they had affected me.

Angel and Jayne had a longer, deeper friendship with Annie, but perhaps they were giving her something *she* needed, too—something akin to what I needed. Perhaps I wasn't such a freak after all. Could Annie be feeling it too? Was she asking herself the love-and-work question?

Fame is a young person's game. I'd never discourage the young from arriving at fame through excellence in their art. But I was older now, and it was time to wise up.

And wise up I did.

I was a lucky person. I had two new friends willing to stand among the thousands just for me. They were *my* people, my true fans, and I was a fan of theirs. And I had Nestor, who was grown-up enough to see it all, stop what he was doing, and lead me to them. He saw what I needed and did what he could to provide it.

On that awful day of self-doubt, I realized my sore spot hadn't healed as much as I had hoped. I still had work to do. But I had dear, beloved people in my life who wouldn't hesitate to swoop in to help me—people like Nestor, Jayne, and Angel. What more could I ask for?

I did ask for more, however. I asked for the opportunity to be there in all the days to come, whenever they needed me to help *them*.

Chapter Sixteen

FEBRUARY 2010

An empty bed doesn't bother me a bit. Touching another living being is my recipe for a sleepless night. My children, at a very young age, were a welcome and necessary exception to this rule. Otherwise, I can only sleep if my body is completely unencumbered by anyone's touch.

My friend Barb, on the other hand, doesn't sleep well in an empty bed. I sometimes wondered whether there was an underlying reason for our opposing sleep dispositions. If so, why wasn't I the one burdened with a husband who was away from home? That guilt finally slid away when I learned Barb's husband Joe was returning home from almost a year in Afghanistan—as did my fear she might lose him.

Since I'd met Barb, every time I'd heard that an American helicopter had crashed in Afghanistan, I'd say a prayer of hope that Joe hadn't been on board. And I'd feel relieved when Barb appeared that afternoon or the next day at school, happy and smiling.

The army had given Joe short pockets of decompression time on his trip back from Afghanistan. He'd seen counselors on the US base in Germany (the usual protocol), and he'd also been debriefed on American soil. Then, with just a few days' notice, Barb was given his flight details so she and the kids could be at the airport to welcome him home.

I hadn't seen Barb in a few weeks while her family took some time alone to reconnect. Then one afternoon at the end of February, when I was parked at my usual spot by the Le Jardin Academy sports field, waiting for Rafa to finish soccer practice, I heard a *tap, tap, tap* on my window. I jumped out of my daydreams and turned to find Barb.

The soccer field is perched on the top tier of the little layered school—any higher, and it would be carved into the Koʻolau mountains, which loom over it like a kind giant assigned to protect the tiny children. I had been gazing up at the mountains, my head tilted so far back my jaw hung loose, thinking about how not a day went by without me getting lost for a moment in the island's graceful strength and beauty.

"Joe's here," Barb whispered giddily when I rolled down the window. "You have to meet him!"

Barb had been incredibly strong throughout Joe's deployment, especially so because she's the kind of woman who thrives in her partnership. It wasn't that Barb always spoke about Joe, but just that somehow he slipped seamlessly into any conversation about her life, and always with warmth. Joe was always around her, even when he wasn't there.

There was one particular day when I'd felt Barb's solitude. She'd been getting some work done for a school fundraising gala while I minded her kids. When she came to pick them up, she seemed different. Strapping Allie into her car seat, she said to me, "I'd planned on quieting down and trying to look inward while Joe is gone."

Until then, I'd never seen her look so unsettled about Joe being away. She seemed so lost—tired, yet in a hurry. I gave her a quick hug, and she brushed some hair from her forehead and then blotted the sweat with the back of her hand.

"I'm kind of doing the opposite," she continued with a deep sigh. "I never stop."

It was the first time she had fully, albeit briefly, shared her pain with me. And then she was off.

Now Barb's heroic husband was home, and I had to get out of the car and give him a hug. But I was still in my pajama pants. I'd never intended to leave my vehicle that afternoon. My top was dirty because I'd procrastinated on the housework, done it all at the last minute, and worked up a sweat, leaving no time to slip on a new one. I'd also put off brushing my hair and cleaning my teeth.

My procrastination had bitten me in the ass.

For a long time, I'd been dying to meet Joe, dying to thank him for his bravery and sacrifice and service to our country—dying to gush about how much I adored his wife and how I'd instantly felt akin to her, about how his kids had the most lovely nature and the most beautiful manners I'd ever seen in children that age. I'd heard it said that military families were literally working for their country and its freedom and for the world by extension. They were truly earning their place in

America. I'd always been in awe of that sense of purpose. Now I was witnessing it firsthand. There was nothing between Barb and Joe but the purity of that goal.

On this day, that truth screamed especially loudly. To me, it was clear I was taking my life for granted, whereas Barb was truly earning hers.

Barb had put value in partnership and purpose and motherhood at an early age. She'd met Joe in her first year of college, and by her early twenties she was vowing before family and friends that she'd partner with him for the rest of her life. Having received her biggest gift quite early in life, she had been grateful ever since.

I'd spent my twenties quite differently, with some great friendships and just a few boyfriends. I'd been so driven to succeed as an actress that I gave partnering the back seat. I never really did what should've come naturally at that age—exploring intimate relationships. Unlike Barb, I had taken for granted that I'd find my partner eventually. I was lucky I did.

For Barb, having a family was an aspiration. She shouldn't have been living her days unsure as to whether she'd see Joe at the airport in a year or be left holding a tiny folded American flag. Those doubts and questions should've been reserved for someone like me—someone who thought having a family was something she'd get around to one day . . . maybe.

❦

I know the exact moment I went from thinking, *I'll probably have a family of my own* to thinking, *Well, maybe that won't happen for me.* The switch flipped when I was twenty-two years old, watching a production of Henrick Ibsen's *A Doll's House*. The play ends with its lead character, Nora, returning her wedding ring and house keys to her husband before walking out on him and their three children. As Nora slammed the door behind her and the curtain went down, I found myself weeping hard, on the verge of blubbering.

The lights went up quickly, and I looked around me. Nobody else in the theater had been emotionally affected as I had. The old theater saying, "There was not a dry eye in the house" had been flipped to "There was not a *wet* eye in the house, except for that crazy girl in the cheap seats." I pulled it together fast.

It had been a good production, straightforward and clear—the kind of unpretentious show that allows the playwright's words to shine. Right before Nora leaves, she tells her husband how she feels: She has been treated like a doll her whole life, like a plaything and not a person, first by her father and then by him. She needs to leave in order to find out who she really is, so she can decide what to do with her future. When he professes his love for her, she argues he has never loved her true self but only the role she has played.

My empathy for Nora's struggle had no feminist agenda. As a young woman, I was benefiting from the feminist movement, but I was in no way influenced by it. I read later that Ibsen himself had said, "[I] must disclaim the honor of having consciously worked for the women's rights movement." He had been simply in service of a "description of humanity."

It was Ibsen's tale of humanity, of Nora's humanity, that had floored me. All the plot twists that lead up to those final moments force Nora to face her deepest truth—her humanity at its purest. She realizes something is so amiss in her life that in order to live in it truthfully, she has no choice but to leave her family—and shockingly, her children—in order to preserve her own humanness. The better choice for her is to be alone.

Nora's final scene is almost too heartbreaking to bear. As actors, we are taught to be truth-tracking machines, and when we uncover a character's soul, the *ping, ping, ping* is powerful and mesmerizing. Once actors hook into a character's center, they never forget it—perhaps because often it has something to do with their own self at its purest form. Nora's goal is to be seen honestly as a whole being and not for the role she has long been expected to play.

This resonated with the twenty-two-year-old me. At that age, I was a lonely person, far from home—far from any kind of romantic love. Watching the play, I realized that success in my personal life might be as unattainable as the success I was chasing in my professional world. What if there was nobody out there who would be truly happy with me—the real me, with all of my messy humanness? What if the only way for me to be a good partner was to pretend, like Nora, to be something I was not?

I knew myself too well by then. Drama school had taught me to act truthfully under imaginary circumstances, not to fake it. I had pulled out many dark parts of myself in order to play different people. I was open emotionally, although not yet in control of my emotions. I suspected I might be too much for any guy to take on. But there was no going back. The idea of faking it in order to make someone love me was unfathomable.

I had yet to discover what healthy compromise in a relationship meant, let alone what a healthy relationship even was. But the demands of drama school—to investigate one's deepest self—were making me fragile and wary. My fear was so overwhelming that when the Ibsen play was over and I pulled myself together, I decided it would be best to stick to my goal of acting and not think of a "happily ever after." And I didn't . . . mostly.

As time went on, I grew accustomed to functioning as a solitary human. Still, sometimes in my darkest failures on the audition trail, I allowed myself to fantasize that I might find love and have children one day—as a consolation prize. I gave myself the hope there would be more for me than just acting. But then I'd have a good streak and book some jobs, and I'd quickly forget about ever having a family.

All those mind games ended when I met Nestor.

Several years after blubbering over *A Doll's House*, I looked into Nestor's eyes, and a wave of comfort washed over me. A full sense of relief would come later, but on that first day I was simply reassured to find a fellow castmate who was as terrified as I was.

We were two of eleven young actors cast in the *Muscle* pilot, which had already been picked up and guaranteed to air on The WB. We were at our first table reading, in front of a hundred or so executives—studio, network, agency, management—a lot of suits who filled the air with a high-stakes, nervous energy. For me, that energy was contagious.

When performing a drama, actors can allow their nerves to seep into the characters' emotional motivation. At times, when the stakes are serious, an actor's nerves can even create a little shimmer around their performance. But in comedy, nobody should see you sweat. A stressed-out comedic actor unsettles an audience, and an unsettled audience does not laugh. Also, nobody laughs less than a room full of executives.

Many of the other actors were full of bravado. They were witty and loose and looked genuinely happy to be there. Perhaps their gratitude for the job had trumped every other emotion. Or maybe they just had great comedic energy. Either way, I admired their style and their authenticity. I just didn't play that way. Despite my training as an actor, I couldn't pretend in real life. My gratitude after scoring this sitcom job had quickly turned to fear—fear of failing, fear of being fired. Only once the script was open and the reading or acting started did I stand a chance of conquering my terror.

On that very first morning of the job, everyone was milling around a buffet table set up on the cavernous sound stage where we'd be shooting the show. Aside from being devoid of natural light and air, sound stages are often chilled to Siberian coldness. Meanwhile, the playing areas (where the sets are built) blaze with thousands of lights, while the offstage areas remain dark. I was dying to step into the black, but I knew I had to mill around the most brightly lit breakfast buffet on earth and nibble on my bagel as though I were at some kind of merry, madcap cocktail party.

That's where I locked eyes with Nestor. I'd seen his photo on the cast sheet. He was directly across the buffet from me, reaching for some food. He wasn't smiling. He had nothing clever to say. He simply looked at me pointedly, as though to make sure I knew he was just as scared as I was.

The moment went by quickly, but I'll never forget his eyes that day. They felt like home. His eyes would be the eyes of my children—different shades of brown, but old eyes, deep eyes, honest eyes that seemed to inhabit the same world as me. I had met my family.

From the time we met, it took Nestor and me seven years to walk down the aisle. Those years were loving and fun, but clunky. All my time being single had given me a specific idea about how a relationship should be. I had lofty notions with little experience. Plus, we come from profoundly different cultures; his parents are Cuban exiles who mostly speak Spanglish in their house. I'm from Australia, where, growing up, I'd never even encountered a Latin immigrant.

The small bumps along our path seemed to me even more difficult to navigate than the big roadblocks. For instance, Nestor was clumsy with delicate objects in my apartment. He seemed to always be coming over with super glue or a hammer and nails to fix whatever he'd broken. I find it funny now, but back then—when I had little spare change and I treasured those few objects—it irritated me. I wasn't sure if I could live with that forever. Also, I was a free spirit, while he was a protective Latin lover. I could never understand why he begged me to wear a bra. I thought these small issues would add up to our future demise. But they never did.

There was nothing at Nestor's core that felt wrong to me. Everything about him felt right. I knew I had to get my act together.

I went to therapy, tried to shed my misconceptions about love, and accelerated my on-the-job relationship training. I didn't want to lose the best person who'd ever come into my life. I'd grown up dreaming of being an actress, not a homemaker, but once I met Nestor, I wanted a traditional "happily ever after."

Though it worked out for Nestor and me, I always wish I could've offered him more grace in the beginning—more amiability, more patience, and the kind of unending devotion he showed me. I owed it to him, because he was in love with me and I was in love with him, and it was a good love for both of us. Nestor, who has kindness and elegance to spare, deserved that grace.

✿

Years later in Hawaii, when I met Barb, I couldn't help but be reminded of my shortcomings as a family person. When she told me she always slept with a part of her body touching Joe's, I marveled at how she'd been physically conditioned for partnership. Like a swimmer endowed with a tall, lean build, huge hands for water grasp, and extra lung capacity, Barb was made for marriage and motherhood, and she filled that role with grace. I was the opposite—clumsy at both of those jobs.

Every so often I'd need, with every fiber of my being, to take a few days away from Nestor and the kids. My friends in LA joked about my "me-cations," but it was more complicated than that. Rather than yearn for a massage or a facial or a nice meal, I needed solitude.

Two hours into my drive, of course, I'd miss all three of my guys. Nostalgia would get the better of me—I'd be overcome with a wistful, almost tearful homesickness at the thought of them going about their day without me—especially when Nestor helpfully assured me they were doing great and having a fantastic time. But after a day, I'd be good. After two days,

I'd be great, beginning to cherish my isolation. I fell into the rhythm of being alone very easily.

I couldn't help but wonder: Was my need for solitude a defect in my personality, a part of my growth I had purposely retarded in my twenties?

One day, Rikke and I dropped into Barb's place while she was Skyping with Joe. She wanted me to "meet" him, so she hurried us inside and over to the computer. There he was from the chest up, open and smiling. It was like looking into a crystal ball and seeing young Joey in the future: a disciplined boy with a fun heart, good humor, and the same deep-set and piercing eyes.

I awkwardly popped in frame, said hi to Joe, and then popped out. I'm sure I laughed too loudly.

Rikke and I gasped like schoolgirls when Joe blew Barb a kiss goodbye that was direct and manly, with the slightest sense of yearning. It was sort of breathtaking. Barb just beamed. I felt a jolt of envy.

I'd felt that envy toward Barb for quite some time. She could cook up flawless dishes with trendy ingredients like orzo and quinoa. She jogged almost every day. She headed up the fundraising committee at school. I admired her in a fantastical way at first, as if she were a fairy princess. But as I got to know her and she became more human, I liked her even more—and my envy grew. I envied her purpose, which was clear-cut, and her stakes, which were high.

And I believed she was more deserving of the comfort a family brings than I was. As a younger woman, I had investigated the darkest parts of myself in order to serve a craft of make-believe, and the residual effects had caused me to approach my real life with great fear and apprehension. Barb, on the other hand, was building her real-life, grown-up family. I had found my family as a lucky consolation prize, but hers was her destiny, and when Joe was away, her destiny was on shaky ground.

No wonder she was giddy at the soccer field parking lot after being without him for almost a year.

"You have to meet him!" she said again happily, clapping her hands.

"Oh yes," I answered with glee. Secretly, though, I was bummed. I didn't want to meet Joe in my pajamas.

I stepped out of the car.

Aside from being handsome—Barb later explained there was no drinking on base and not much to do in one's downtime in Afghanistan except lose a bunch of weight, work out a lot, and get really buff—Joe seemed so lovely. He approached me with a big smile and outstretched arms, and all I could do was pull my whole self back into my bones while I hugged him, keeping my braless boobs well away from him. I just hoped that he couldn't smell my breath or my body odor, and that he wouldn't look down and notice my checkered pajama pants. We exchanged "Nice to meet yous" and "I've heard so much about yous," but I just couldn't reach out to him in the way I wanted.

Barb was aflush with happiness, but I felt awful. I should have been taking Joe in fully—really seeing him in the way Barb deserved, with an approach that was open and available. Instead I was in so much disarray I couldn't even look him in the face.

Thankfully, the kids ran over and saved me. Joey and Allie

jumped on their dad, and Joey kept checking back in with Rafa, excited to show off his dad to his friend. The kids were pink-faced and flushed, with a soft layer of sweat from soccer practice. Barb and Joe were smiling and content. The five of them looked golden. I felt bad pulling Rafa away from the beautiful tableau and leading him to our minivan.

Driving back to the house, I began to wonder what was wrong with me. Why had I let myself be so gross all day? When I was an actress, I was on top of everything. I looked the best I could. I was well prepared for auditions and on time for work, and I knew my characters' lines forward and backward. But as a mom I was always five minutes late, perpetually putting off cleaning, grocery shopping, and cooking. Often I didn't have time to wash myself or change my clothes. What had happened to the little bit of grace I had acquired over the years? It had gotten lost, along with the value of my purpose.

That night, after the kids were asleep, I had a moment with Nestor. He was on our bed, working on his lines—not the best time for a talk. When Nestor has scenes to shoot the next day, he becomes single-minded about his job. He works in fear that he is only as good as the last scene he shoots. It's a typical actor mindset, a way to assert control in a career that gives very little guarantee of when the next paycheck will come. But I needed him in that moment, so I sat down beside him anyway.

"I have to talk to you," I said.

"I have to work on this material," he groaned. "I have very little to do in this episode, and I don't want to make too much of it."

"I really need to talk," I insisted.

He shook his head. "And I have to work."

We were practically in a fight before the conversation began. "Nestor," I said, almost in tears. "I *really* need to talk."

"All right, all right," he relented.

I paused, feeling a big sigh build in my chest as I looked down at the bright, traditional Hawaiian quilt on our bed, which I found gaudy at first but had come to love. "What do you like about me?"

Nestor began to shift on the bed. I could see he was thinking this might be a long one.

"I'm really serious," I pleaded. "What do you like about me as a wife and a mom?"

"Why are you asking this?"

"I'm just feeling like I'm not bringing that much to the table. I mean, look at Barb. She cooks great meals for her kids and does a lot at the school, and she's so in shape—"

He stopped me. "Why do you have this fascination with Barb?"

"I just feel like she's a really good partner."

"But she's a good partner in the way that you're a good partner," Nestor explained. "People want to be around her the same way they want to be around you—because she just gives of herself. She's right there, ready for you. It's not that other stuff. You have what she has. That's what makes you a good mom. It's what the boys love. Not that you're a good cook or cleaner. It's just that you're with us and you're here for us. It's just you. You give us you. That's what I love about you."

He went back to reading his lines, and I meandered out of the bedroom, heading for the long, stiff couch in the living area—right at the windows, looking out onto the beach. We rarely used this space, as it was more of a formal entertaining nook. I gazed at our two Siamese fighting fish, Speedo and Biggie, in their separate bowls. Nestor was right about Barb— the reason I felt at home with her was because she was open and available, willing to connect and to give her unique self. That's what I loved about her. And Nestor loved the same thing in me. Maybe I wasn't great at some of the stuff around the periphery of being a mom and a wife, but I did love being there face-to-face with him and the kids. I loved connecting with them.

Over the seven months we had been in Hawaii, the hole in my chest had been slowly shrinking. I was proud of that, but I'd forgotten something along the way: The most important part of partnering was showing up for my little tribe.

He's right. I am doing that, I thought. *Oh, thank God. I actually do that!*

It was such a relief and so simple, really, but it was true and it was enough. I may not have an overabundance of grace, but I was built for the ones who love me. I have all the grace they need.

Chapter Seventeen

FEBRUARY 2010

E veryone knows a ringing phone at 4 a.m. means bad news—an accident or even the sudden death of someone you love. But when the phone rang before dawn on February 27, I wasn't too worried. It was the rental house landline, which we rarely used. People we love knew how to contact us: on our LA cell phones with the numbers we'd had for years.

It's for a previous renter, I surmised, slowly opening my eyes. *Bad news for them? Nah. Probably not. Back to sleep.*

When the phone rang again twenty minutes later, I made the same assumption. If I were to get out of bed, walk through the living room to the little office alcove behind the kitchen, and answer the phone, I'd fully wake up. It was Saturday, and I'd planned a big day for my energetic boys. While Nestor was in Los Angeles doing some press for *LOST*, we were going to hike, swim, boogie board, and skim board. My hope was to wear them out by day's end like a pair of puppies. I'd need my sleep.

About fifteen minutes later, the phone rang again. It was now 4:40 a.m., and I was beginning to wonder and worry. Someone really *could* be dead.

My eyes popped open. I needed to call Nestor.

I reached for my cell and tried to turn it on, but the battery was drained.

Oh, that's right, I thought. Nestor had accidentally taken both chargers with him to LA. I'd been unable to power up my phone the night before. I felt the flush of frustration and started getting annoyed all over again. Nestor's head was so often in the clouds, and whenever he disrupted the order in my life, I became disproportionately angry—and afterward, guilty about my hot temper.

Then it occurred to me: If I wasn't answering my cell phone, the caller was most likely trying the house phone.

My anger shifted to panic.

Shit!

I ran out to the living room, which was washed in late blue moonlight blended with the faint beginnings of early orange sunlight. I had never been up that early in Kailua and, even in a moment of high stress, I was transfixed by the colors beaming off that ocean. It was as though an infinite color wheel lived beneath those waters.

Forcing my eyes away from the windows, I moved toward the house phone. Thank goodness, Nestor picked up right away. "Hey, babe." He sounded relaxed and a bit groggy.

"Have you been calling?" I asked. "What's going on?"

"Yes." He was mellow, so I immediately relaxed until he said, "A tsunami is going to hit the island."

"What?" I tried to compute this news. "Seriously? When?"

"Around 11:30 a.m. your time," he answered. "You've got to get to high ground."

11:30? "You couldn't have waited a little to call?" It was so early—and a disaster expected to happen in six hours didn't really feel like a disaster.

"I know, I know," he replied. "I thought the same thing, but my parents scared me."

Nestor's mom and dad live in Connecticut, five hours ahead, and had awoken to the news that a massive 8.8 earthquake had rocked Chile. Hundreds of deaths had been reported, and a tsunami was gathering speed and heading our way.

"Oh, no," I said quietly, thinking about Haiti. "Another one."

"You have a lot of time," Nestor said. "Don't panic. I'll call you later." He hung up, and I was sure he went back to sleep . . . in his comfy bed . . . in his dark, cozy room . . . at the Four Seasons . . .

Pushing my resentment aside, I realized I had a lot to get my head around. Taking a deep breath, I looked out at the ocean again, which appeared incredibly flat and peaceful.

Holy crap, I thought. *The neighbors were right.*

When I first met the Cartwrights, our neighbors next door, I assumed they were on a great adventure. They had been moving all around the US and experiencing the most alluring places to raise their family. The more we began to know them, however, the more I realized they weren't so carefree after all. Mother Nature's power over the island frightened them. Nervous about riptides, they rarely took their kids down to the ocean. The jellyfish, giant leaping cane spiders, and huge centipedes worried them constantly and kept them indoors.

I was familiar with such fears but not exactly sympathetic. Growing up in Australia, we were always outdoors. If we happened upon a deadly creature and ran home scared, we were told to go back outside and just be careful. "Stop being ridiculous," our parents would say.

The Cartwrights frustrated me. Here I was, savoring every moment on Oʻahu, with the sad knowledge that our time here was almost over. Meanwhile, they were analyzing and assessing life in Kailua so they could figure out whether they wanted to stay or leave. Where I was seeing only rainbows, the Cartwrights were wondering if they wanted to live with all the rain showers.

One day, when I revealed how much I enjoyed living right on the beach, they shook their heads vehemently. Their rental was one house back from the ocean, toward the street. That's when they told me they'd never buy beachfront property, because of tsunamis.

That's crazy, I thought. The chances of a deadly tsunami happening in Hawaii are so unlikely. It would take a sizeable earthquake in a specific location for one to hit. The stars would have to align in precisely the wrong way.

After an awkward pause, I just said, "Oh," and nodded my head. Then I laid a big, fat, silent judgment upon them for choosing to live in fear. They were perfectly lovely people, but their choices repelled me.

The truth was, however, I'd been fighting my own fears since I was a child, and I couldn't afford any add-ons.

I'm not sure when my anxiety began, but my first big moment of fear happened after a bridge collapsed in 1975 in Tasmania, the little triangular island that sits below Australia's southeastern coast. A boat crashed into a pier that supported the bridge, causing the road above to break in two. Four cars could not stop in time. I didn't have *all* of those details; I was only seven years old. But I heard my mum and dad talking about the cars falling and the people dying. It sounded terrifying, and I developed a fear of bridges.

I didn't tell a soul about the horror I felt—not even when we took the Sydney Harbour Bridge every week to visit my grandparents for dinner. As we drove across the enormous steel "Coat Hanger," I'd wedge my face in the little valley made by the curves of the cushioned back seat and stare cross-eyed at the pale brown stitching. The drive across the bridge was long, a four-lane highway in both directions.

Please keep us safe, I prayed to God the whole time.

One day, about a year after the Tasmanian bridge collapsed, I was playing on the grass in an area on the north side of Sydney, right under the Harbour Bridge—directly in front of one of the huge pylons. Four pylons in total held up the bridge, each the size of a large tower and made of giant light-colored sandstones laid out interlocking like bricks. I walked all the way around the pylon, and to me it looked as big as a castle. I stared up at the bridge and the enormous pylon, spotted the identical pylon across the harbor, and realized there was no way on earth this immense bridge would ever fall down. My worries had been unwarranted. I was never scared to cross it again.

I had other fears as a child—hundreds of others. And over the past few months in Hawaii, Nestor and I had seen something in Marco, something that concerned Nestor but for me was like looking in a mirror: Marco was developing fears, and it wasn't just his "soldier in 'Nam" bit whenever the wind suddenly slammed a door shut.

Walking down to Waimea Bay one day for a boogie board ride, we saw the waves were unusually large, breaking on the shore with a ferocity that was new to me. A man was being taken off the beach in a stretcher, and another was hobbling out of the surf with blood dripping down his forehead, which explained the ambulance in the parking lot. Other beachgoers warned us to stay on shore and keep the kids out of the water.

Later, when Rafa and his little buddy started playing a game of chase with the last bits of white water rolling on the sand, Marco became hysterical, screaming for me to keep Rafa away. Seeing his brother in what he perceived as danger was torturing him. He was inconsolable, so we left the beach early that day.

As Nestor drove us away from the beach, I patted Marco's white dimply knee. I had a feeling his childhood might be cursed with worries like mine. "I'll watch him like a hawk," I said to Nestor. "And I won't let him keep it to himself like I did."

I felt so sad for Marco, and so guilty. It wasn't his fault. I'd probably passed this behavior down on some random chromosome, or perhaps he had somehow absorbed it from my actions. Thinking I had caused his future pain made my heart sink for him under the weight of a sorrow so overpowering the world stopped for a minute. But then I looked at his face, shiny and smooth from the sunscreen, and saw he was already beaming and laughing out loud at something silly Rafa was doing. His little Chiclet teeth made him look so innocent, so happy and carefree. I silently vowed to help make it different for him somehow.

That day as a child under the Harbour Bridge pylons in Sydney had taught me to think my fears through in an analytical way. It was hard work, and I was in my head all the time, thinking and analyzing and laboring my way to a place of clarity without apprehension. I had built up my own coping mechanisms over the years. But there were times when I was not successful, when my emotions were so strong I couldn't see clearly enough to find any solace. The past few years—my lost years—had been such a time.

I had been finding it incredibly hard to ease the pain of leaving acting. The hole in my chest was too large, and too much of me had fallen through it. I was trying to scoop my sense of self back in and sew up that gaping hole. It was a really scary time, and perhaps that's what bothered me so much about the Cartwrights. I couldn't be around fearful people, because frightened people frightened *me*.

But standing there in our Kailua living room on the morning of February 27, I realized my neighbors' fears were not unfounded. The ocean could destroy this neighborhood I loved so much, made up of friends I'd come to love even more. The very ocean I swam in every day, so far beyond the break that Nestor would call for me to swim in closer—the ocean that had hypnotized me into a fearless love bordering on worship—could destroy everything in just a few hours.

My anxiety began to rise.

I wasn't frightened for our lives. I knew we'd be safe. We had plenty of time to get to high ground. I was worried about the house. I'd grown very attached to our sturdy old Hawaiian lady on the beach. She was frayed around the edges but reliable and airtight. She was our access to the beautiful sea—she allowed us to be with it every day, whether through her generous windows or by stepping down her path onto the beach.

But now the very same sea, which the house proudly sat above like a sphinx, might be her worst enemy. Even a foot of seawater gushing through would cause significant damage. I needed to protect her, to fortify her against the wave.

I needed a plan.

❀

When I turned on the TV news, I saw Nestor was right: Everyone on the coast of every island in the Hawaiian archipelago was instructed to seek high ground well before the first predicted wave at 11:30 a.m. From what I could gather, though, most experts agreed there would be a significant rise in the water level rather than a huge tidal wave.

I started to unplug all the electrical cords from the lower outlets and place everything that was on the floor—chairs, rugs, and any piece of furniture I could lift—on tables or countertops. I emptied the closet floors, took off all the linens and scrunched them in a ball, and placed everything on the beds.

I was able to charge my cell phone through the computer, and once it had some battery life, I saw scores of text messages and a bunch of missed phone calls, not just from Nestor but also from friends who were worried about us. Suddenly, my cell phone rang. It was Dewey—my friend Lili's husband, to whom we had also become close. They lived on a hill street in Kāneʻohe.

"Are you okay, darlin'?" Dewey asked. "I know Nestor's out of town."

"Oh yes. I'm fine. You're so sweet."

"Well, Lili wants you and the boys to come up and be with us. Irene and Scot are coming up, and so are Marc and Rikke."

Rikke and her family had just moved onto the street next to ours, once Marc had finished building their dream home from the ground up. He had worked with his bare hands on his weekends off from his day job helping run a company that installed steel railings on Hawaii's many hotel balconies. The man worked harder than almost anyone I'd ever seen, hauling and hammering and digging and doing stuff that left him red and drenched with sweat. Whenever I'd walk past the house, I'd call out to him and wave. He would smile and wave back, and as he'd raise his head, the perspiration would fly off his hair like sea spray. What an incredible blow a flood would be to Marc and Rikke! They still had boxes everywhere and had invested years in a house that could now be damaged by a single wave.

"Oh God," I said to Dewey. "Marc and Rikke. Are they okay?"

"They're fine," he answered quickly. "It'll be nothing. We'll barbecue. The kids can play. We'll have fun. Good thing your friends are hill dwellers."

Dewey was just as kind and fun as Lili. At Rafa's soccer practice once, before I officially met them, I saw a couple sitting on the sidelines and eating sandwiches. Lili looked up at me, smiled, and said, "This must be the most beautiful soccer field in the world, right?"

I struck up a short conversation and learned they'd both taken a late lunch from work so they could watch their kids, Stella and Campbell, practice. That was Lili and Dewey: hard workers who devoted every free moment to being with their kids and celebrating life with friends. They organized lots of days at the beach, nights out to dinner, and barbecues with the children. There were no better people to hole up with on tsunami day.

"Thanks, Dewey," I said. "We'll come up." I was texting a quick explanation of our plan to Barb, Angel, and my other friends when the sirens started to blare.

We'd first heard the sirens early in our stay, while visiting Sunset Beach up on the North Shore. They weren't terribly loud, just loud enough to make it confusing as to whether they were being sounded for a specific purpose. At first I thought they were shark alarms like we used to have when I was a kid, swimming in Sydney—although these were too soft to hear out in the surf. Then the lifeguard sitting atop the tall wooden stand explained we were hearing the tsunami warning testing system that sounded all along the coast on the first day of every month. In the months that followed, I occasionally heard the alarms, but I never thought anything of it.

That morning of the tsunami, the blaring sirens were significantly louder and lasted longer than those muted tests. It was 6 a.m. by then, and I knew they'd wake up the boys, so I rushed into their room.

"Okay, guys," I said, smothering them with the usual morning kisses, kisses they'd invariably wipe off their faces. "Don't be frightened by the sirens. It's actually pretty exciting. We have a tsunami warning. A real one!" I sped on. "It's going to be fun. We're going to drive up to Stella and Campbell's house, have breakfast and a barbecue, and play all day."

"A *what* warning?" Rafa asked suspiciously.

"A tsunami warning. A big-wave warning," I said cheerfully. "It just means a big wave might come and get the house a little bit wet."

I could see Marco wasn't buying my casual tone. In fact, he was beginning to panic. So I picked him up in my arms and repeated the plan to him, gushing about what a great day we were going to have. Then I took him to the bathroom to pee, popped him in front of the TV (careful to avoid any news), and turned on his favorite cartoon channel.

"I'm here and I'm just gonna get things organized, but I'll come anytime you call," I told him. "And if there's anything to worry about, I'll tell you, because I know what it's like to worry. But there's really nothing to worry about, because we have tons of time and the only *real* worry is the floor might get wet. So I have to get things up off the floor—that's all."

Somewhere in the middle of my speech, the sirens stopped and Marco's attention strayed to the TV, so I got on with things. I was at the fridge, figuring out what food I should take up to Dewey's, when the doorbell rang.

There was Gabby Cartwright standing in front of me, with the family car pulled up behind her in our circular driveway.

She was pale and breathless. "Nestor left a message with me because you weren't answering your phone. He asked me to check in on you." Before I could get a word in, she told me she was glad we were awake. She motioned with her head toward the car and added, "We're getting the hell out of here."

As I started to reassure her, telling her we had hours before the wave would hit, her husband began honking his horn loudly. She bolted back into the car, and he peeled away with a screech of tires, leaving a small dust cloud behind them.

How nice of them to check in on me, I thought, especially considering the stress they seemed to be under. Then I wondered if I'd ever see them again. Perhaps this tsunami would be the deciding factor in their dilemma about whether or not Kailua was the best place in America to live. If I were to hear they'd headed straight to the airport and sent for their stuff later, I wouldn't have been surprised.

As I turned to go back inside the house, I was startled to find both boys standing directly behind me, wide-eyed and a little confused. They had come with me to the door and witnessed the whole exchange.

The usually quiet street was starting to feel chaotic. A police car drove by with loudspeakers calling out a warning: A mandatory evacuation was in place, and everyone must leave their homes and head for higher ground. That awful, ear-piercing feedback from the microphone was more jarring than the actual message.

All of this sent Marco into a panic.

He began to run around in circles, screaming and asking if the wave was coming. I tried to calm him. Only when I implored him to look out at the sea was he reassured. The sun had risen over the tranquil, flat ocean, and the water had become its famous Kailua aqua, looking as unthreatening as I'd ever seen it.

"We have hours yet," I said nonchalantly, so practiced in giving reasonable answers to unfounded fears. "And the wave is only going to be tiny. Just big enough to maybe wet the floor."

I silently cursed the police for being so dramatic. Or did they know something we weren't being told? The sirens were about to go off again—it was all too unsettling—so I suggested to the boys we just leave now. After loading our food in the trunk, we were about to get in the minivan and take off when I heard a shriek nearby. My heart practically vaulted out of my chest.

"SHANNON! Are you all right?"

It was my neighbor, wailing from the other side at the back corner of the fence. She lived on the street over to the north, and I had met her down on the beach. We'd chatted several times. I didn't know much about her, except that she lived with her husband and their two grown-up sons, all of whom I'd yet to meet.

"Oh! Hi, Margaret," I answered, gathering my breath. "We're good. Is everything okay with you?"

"Ah! I don't know!" She wailed again, and then in a low, ominous voice she said, "Oh, you don't even know. This tsunami is the least of our problems."

It was strange. She'd always been so upbeat on the beach.

"Oh. Umm, I'm sorry. Ah . . . can I do anything?" I asked weakly.

"Ugh, no," she said distractedly and shuffled away.

"Crazy, right?" I called to her.

"Yep. Take care." Her voice trailed off, and I noticed the boys were standing right behind me yet again, silent and with eyes even bigger than before.

"Is this a nutso day or what?" I said to them cheerfully. And it was. Every event was unfolding one minute after the other, as though we were in a movie. "Come on, let's go."

I tuned the car radio to a news station and started out for Kāneʻohe. Within a minute, there was a crackle and a long beep as President Obama came on the airwaves, advising the people of Hawaii to stay calm and follow all emergency instructions.

This can't be real, I thought, feeling like Tom Cruise in *War of the Worlds*, driving his kids to safety, only it was a wave rather than aliens nipping at our heels. And yet as we rounded the curve, there was Kāneʻohe Bay, as gorgeous and sparkly as Kailua Beach had been, with not even a ripple in sight.

"We're missing a fantastic day on the beach," I exclaimed and immediately felt a flash of guilt. Was I being too flippant? Maybe bad things were about to happen after all. It had been a long strange morning, and it was all so confusing.

Was there going to be a big wave . . . a small wave . . . or no wave at all?

We were the first to arrive at Lili and Dewey's, followed by Irene, Scot, and their boys. Marc, Rikke, and their kids came soon after—Rikke was in a cranky mood. She was scared, of course, but cranky seemed to be a better go-to emotion for her. Rikke is a big softie, and I think she often plays the cranky mood for laughs. She vents inappropriately with deadpan seriousness, and yet, when I tease her, she is quick to set free her gorgeous laugh.

Marc told me he'd stopped by our house to turn off the gas and something else. I had no idea what he was talking about or how he knew where to find the things to turn off, but I hugged him and thanked him for being so sweet. He seemed a little thrown by my sentimentality, perhaps unaware of how much I treasured our house—and how much I'd grown to love his wife and family and him, and all of our friends.

At 11 a.m., we decided to drink mimosas and watch the news as we waited for the wave. A dramatic reporter stood by some brown water he identified as the Wailuku River, which flows into Hilo Bay on the Big Island—the island predicted to be hit first. Hilo had experienced the biggest tsunamis in the islands' modern history, including one in 1946 that caused tremendous damage and the loss of 159 lives.

The TV camera was fixed on a whitewater swirl between some rocks at the river's edge, to demonstrate how the waves came in and receded back into the ocean, tsunami style. The problem was that the camera rarely cut away from this close-up. The few times it did pull out to a wide shot, we could see several ducks having a ball as they surfed along with the stronger current. Sitting there and watching the brown water so closely while listening to the running commentary of an excited reporter, we found it difficult to gain perspective.

"Here it comes, here it comes," someone in our group shouted in earnest. We all shushed each other and watched the screen. The water swirled again and then . . . nothing. We all sat in silence, our heads cocked and our eyes squinted. Was something meant to happen? Or had something happened already, and we didn't catch it?

In the end, it was a little like staring at a dirty toilet bowl.

The theatrical reporter appeared again and again. Each time, we'd all talk some more and then shift our attention back to the dirty water. We'd get quiet again, and wait and watch, and so on and so on. After a while, it became humorous. I found myself secretly rooting for the wave. I almost said so out loud, but that would've made Rikke *really* cranky, so I practiced some rare self-restraint.

The mandatory evacuation was called off a few hours later, and we rang Nestor to tell him all was well. Marc had already lost patience with the curfew and ridden his bike back to our neighborhood to turn the gas back on. But there was no reason to leave. We were enjoying ourselves, so once Marc returned, we all ate dinner at Lili and Dewey's.

As we drove home that night, I realized something: We had found an 'ohana.

In Hawaiian, 'ohana means "family." We have good friends in Los Angeles who, after many years, have become like family. And yet there was something special about the size, the isolation, and the essence of the island that allowed us to make those kinds of meaningful friendships on O'ahu in just a single year.

That morning, we had received eight offers in total from friends on the island, inviting us to seek refuge in their homes. Eight! I had never felt so accepted, so known and loved, by people who were so new in my life. Friendships evolved and grew daily, but the forming of our 'ohana felt more like an event. This gift, this encircling, this feeling of warm encapsulation by an authentic 'ohana was making it almost impossible to feel lost.

Passing the house of our fearful neighbors, I noticed they weren't home yet. It occurred to me the Cartwrights were most likely lost, just as I was. It's why they were so scared of so many things, and it's why I was so scared of them. A lost person can't hold on to other lost people.

The Cartwrights weren't running from adventure to adventure. They were just running scared. I felt a wave of compassion for them—and a smaller one for myself. Perhaps they had not found their 'ohana. And while we had found ours, on an island we loved, it was almost time for us to leave.

Pulling into our garage, I wanted to kick myself. I had fallen blindly in love, and falling in love meant loss—and I'd failed to see it coming.

"Love is God's mistake"—or so I'd learned long ago from that great *Tears for Fears* song. The lyric had resonated with me ever since a talented theater director chose it as the opening song of her production of *Miss Julie*. I heard it at every rehearsal, and then in eight shows a week for four weeks, as my character and her lover lost each other over the course of the play.

All those years later, I realized while sitting in our Hawaiian garage, I had made so much progress in my search to reconcile myself as "just" a wife and a mom. Part of my healing was made possible because I'd stumbled into love—the love of an island and of our new 'ohana. But in doing so, I'd created another problem—another opportunity for loss.

How in the hell was I going to leave?

Chapter Eighteen

APRIL 2010

Everything was coming to a close. Just thinking about the end of our time in Hawaii inflamed my heart with an awful dread that made it feel so large it seemed to snag on the edge of my rib cage each time I inhaled. *LOST* was about to wrap. We'd stay about a month longer so the boys could finish school. Then, like many of the show's cast and crew—and like some of the *LOST* characters themselves—we'd be leaving the island behind us.

I'd always known our time there was finite. Oʻahu is a transitory place, partly due to its large military population but also because of the nature of island living. At the close of every school year, Barb had told me, someone in her family was usually forced to say goodbye to a close friend. Many people suffered from island fever and felt the need to escape. They often referred to Oʻahu as "the rock," as in "I have to get off this rock." But I never felt suffocated by the rock—not even close. The boys and I hadn't set foot off the island since we'd arrived almost a year earlier.

The end of a show is usually celebrated with a wrap party. But on a Saturday evening in mid-April, instead of a party, Nestor and I were headed for a beautiful little church at the Sacred Hearts Academy, a private school for girls in Honolulu.

"So, explain to me again why we're going to the church?" I asked Nestor as we wound our way across the surface streets of Waikiki. We were running late to the *LOST* gathering because we'd spent the early evening at a farewell dinner for Irene and Scot. After six years on the island, the navy had given Scot transfer orders for San Diego. Irene was devastated. We wanted to be at the dinner for our friends, so we'd decided to split our time at both events.

"I'm not really sure," Nestor answered. All he could tell me was what Ian had just texted him. "Carlton and Damon are already there. I think we missed their speech."

Carlton Cuse and Damon Lindelof were the executive producers of *LOST.* They had flown in from LA for the filming of a single scene: the final scene of the series finale. The whole cast would be present at the simple but stunning Saint Margaret Mary Chapel. I didn't understand why actors who weren't part of the scene had been asked to the set on a Saturday night along with their wives. We only knew it was important for Nestor to show up.

LOST was famous for its surprising plot twists. In the final episode of every season, the producers would protect the show from any leaks by sharing the last scene with only the actors who were in it—and Nestor wasn't in this one. So, all we knew about the scene in the church was that it involved a lot of the cast, both present and past, and had been given a long shooting window: about ten or twelve hours.

We drove on in silence as "Faith," our whiskey-drinking navigational voice, led us to the old mission-style church. When we arrived, everyone was on their dinner break. Nestor talked to the producers and some of the actors milling around their trailers and snacking at craft service. Curious, I peeked inside the church, but I couldn't really tell what was going on.

I did notice a bunch of old cast members were back from previous seasons and getting their makeup retouched. Sonya Walger was there—Desmond's true love, Penny. So were Ian Somerhalder and Maggie Grace, who played Boone and Shannon in the early seasons. I felt a little rush of excitement, as though I were really at the church within the real *LOST* world.

I could've watched the *LOST* actors for hours, but I didn't want to appear gawky. Nestor sat with Carlton at the dinner setup, so I joined them and we chatted, waiting for something to happen. But nothing ever really did. Nestor just said goodbye and thanked Damon and Carlton and the crew. Once they started to film again, everyone got busy and we left.

Driving home from the set, Nestor and I both felt a sense of finality. His job, our friends, our paradise home—soon it would all be in the past. I was like a child who didn't want to accept it was bedtime, so I tried to keep the *LOST* part alive by questioning Nestor about the scene at the church.

"What was it about?" I asked. "You must have some idea."

"I really don't," he answered. "It must be in the alternate reality, though."

By the end of the show, the story had morphed into a few

alternate realities, occupied by the same characters but in different relationships with each other, sometimes in different time periods. The scene at the church was set in a reality the writers called a "flash sideways"—neither in the future nor in the past. It was where the survivors had waited for each other in death, the afterlife where they were brought back together in different lifelike scenarios. They had created this flash sideways in awareness so they could move on to the next life together. It was a purgatory of sorts. But I didn't know that then.

"Ugh," I whined, staring out the window of our minivan. "I know they were in an alternate reality. That tells me nothing." I was joking but also slightly on edge thinking about our year ending.

"I know," Nestor said. "But how lucky were we to have this?"

"We were so, so lucky," I agreed. "I'm greedy, though. I want more."

"I know," he said again before falling into silence, most likely worrying about where his next job would come from. The *LOST* part of our adventure was over.

Meanwhile, I worried about how I'd wrench myself from our life in Kailua.

❀

As our departure date grew closer and closer, my dread increased. I began to panic. I'd miss the land, our friends, and our day-to-day lives so much it scared me. I simply didn't want to leave.

I'd found a way to heal on the island. It was easy to feel

that now, after a chunk of time away from Los Angeles. I had doubts about being able to bring the less "lost" version of myself back to the mainland. In LA, I had more than a handful of close friends whose company I cherished, and I was looking forward to seeing them. Everything else worried me.

Our house is in Hollywood, and Hollywood is an industry town. It's the place I had come to with my dream of acting, and the place where I had failed. How easy it would be to fall back into my childish notions of self-worth—the idea that being renowned would add significant weight to who I am. I'd grown up so much in Hawaii! The thought of regressing was terrifying.

So with all this on my mind, a few weeks before we were meant to depart, I slipped into an alternate reality of my own. In this reality, we wouldn't leave at all.

There had been an announcement in the industry newspapers that a new TV remake, *Hawaii Five-0*, would soon start shooting on O'ahu. I made Nestor call his manager to see whether there was a role on the show for him. He had reservations about doing a procedural show—or "crime of the week" series—but I bugged him until he made the call.

As we waited to hear back from Nestor's manager, I fed my dream of staying in Hawaii.

While riding my bike, I spied an open house sign for a home on our street. I skidded to the lawn, threw my bike down, and half-sprinted inside the open house without even thinking to take off my helmet. And I began to imagine a wonderful future.

The home was bigger than ours in LA (which we had been renovating during our stay on O'ahu). It was new construction, clean and open. Each boy would get his own bedroom, and we'd have an extra bathroom. It wasn't beachfront, but the backyard had access to a beach path. The front yard was huge and flat, and we could eventually build a pool on it. The house was three times more than we could afford, but other than that, it was perfect!

I curled up with my dream of living in that house in the same way I used to fantasize in my teens about being with a boy I liked. Back then, I'd go through every moment of my time with the boy in my head, second by second, and I'd live through the minutes with more detail than a person could possibly absorb in a real-life interaction. I'd heighten the experience by listening to a track from Spandau Ballet or Wham!—a ballad for an intimate moment we'd share, or an upbeat song for a fun time together. I must've driven Mum and Dad crazy, playing "Wake Me Up Before You Go-Go" on an endless loop in my bedroom. In that same way, I started dreaming of Nestor working on *Hawaii Five-0* and our family relocating to that house for sale.

I'd put my boys in surf camp for the summer. The next school year, Rafa and Joey would join a canoe paddling team. Almost every beach on O'ahu has a canoe club that races other clubs on weekends. I'd convince my girlfriends to join me on the over-forty women's team. We'd paddle out for practice at sunset, our bodies svelte, our arms toned and brown. Sometimes we'd spot sea turtles. Other times we'd fall into a perfect paddling rhythm, and our breathing would allow us to absorb the ocean and the sky like they were a part of us. I'd appreciate the soft air all over again—air that, by then, I'd have started to take for granted.

My alternate reality lasted only a short while. A day or so later, Nestor heard from his manager that *Hawaii Five-0* had offered one of the leads to Daniel Dae Kim, and they didn't want two *LOST* actors on the show. Daniel is a superb actor who played the role of Jin with a timeless quality and the romance of a classic Hollywood leading man, like William Holden or Gregory Peck. It's no easy feat to play a character who doesn't speak English, but he did so with a confident strength. Aside from all that, he is a good man. His wife is sweet and genuine, and his boys were thriving in the local school. They decided to stay, and it was hard not to be happy for them.

It was time to reset my mind. We were leaving, and I had to figure out how to say goodbye.

The house for sale I'd coveted had brand-new hurricane-proofed windows with metal barriers. I knew this feature would please our neighbors, the Cartwrights. The tsunami hadn't driven them off the island after all. They'd decided to stay.

After knocking on their door, I told them about the house. I pitched it hard, and they said they'd take a look at it. The house wasn't ours to begin with, and they eventually would have seen the For Sale signs as they drove down the street, but it still felt as though I were giving away our home.

I envied them. I was jealous they had enough money to buy the house and were able to stay in Hawaii for as long as they pleased. I was especially bitter because their feelings about the island were ambiguous, while I was in a full-blown love affair that was about to end. But giving them the heads-up on the house felt like I was doing a good deed. They had no ill will toward us and in no way deserved my scorn. Strangely enough, it was really nice to picture, with vicarious excitement, the Cartwrights making a home there.

In those last two weeks, I took a few final rides before giving my bike to our babysitter, Brielle, whom we all adored. Before Brielle came for the bike, I kind of patted it when no one was looking, like a horse owner strokes a well-loved horse. That metal and rubber contraption had taken me to places that had opened my heart to some pretty big feelings—feelings that became ideas and even practices. We were still going to Sunday Mass, for goodness' sake.

We took the remaining three bikes to Rikke and Marc, who could use them when friends came to visit. We had purchased a basketball hoop, and the parents of a friend of Marco's strapped it to the roof of their car and took it away for their boys to use. We cleaned Biggie's and Speedo's fishbowls until they sparkled, and then packed up all the fish food and equipment for their new owners: Lili's kids, Stella and Campbell. We put the boys' boogie boards and skim boards out so any friend who visited could claim them.

It was bad luck, we'd learned, to take any ocean remnants away from the island. So we put our collection of big shells in a basket for the boys' friends to keep. I'd bought this strange apothecary jar from a Japanese department store at the Ala Moana mall, containing shrimp called Holoholo that were only found in Hawaii. The inside of the jar was a whole ecosystem that required no care, and the water stayed perfectly clean and clear. The creatures fed off algae on the seaweed and their own shrimp shells, which they shed every three months. I wasn't sure how I was going to get that jar off my hands, but

Rikke's teenage daughter, Ana, loved the tiny curiosity and happily claimed it for her bedroom.

As the house emptied, it became a rental property again and felt less like our home. That helped to solidify in my mind the fact that we were leaving. It prepared me to say goodbye. And when I woke up on our last morning, all that was left were our suitcases in the middle of the floor and one last day.

We had breakfast that morning at a brand-new restaurant called Boots and Kimo's—only it wasn't really brand-new. For years, it had operated as a little hole-in-the-wall opposite the Longs Drugs parking lot, on the road just before Foodland. It had recently relocated to a prime corner on Hekili Street.

Our mystery was solved!

The long line of people outside the unadorned storefront was neither for a pinball palace nor a church meeting but for Boots and Kimo's, a Hawaiian homestyle eatery that had become so popular they moved it to a bigger location. At its new spot on the corner, it *still* had a long line of people waiting to get in. Rumor had it both Betty Crocker and Aunt Jemima had been attempting to buy its macadamia nut pancake sauce recipe, but Boots and Kimo's was holding out. Aside from breakfast, the restaurant still serves a traditional Hawaiian "plate lunch"—two scoops of rice with pork, beef, or chicken, plus a side of macaroni salad. We enjoyed our food in the gleaming new space.

After that, we drove to Kailua Beach Park to watch Joe compete in a canoe regatta. We were led through the parking lot by the smell of barbecue, which provided heavy top notes to the usual scent of sea spray and pine. There were tarpaulins everywhere as people prepared food while they waited for their races. Joe looked intense, stretching and quietly conferencing with his team members. At the start of the race, his team dominated, holding the lead most of the way, only to be overtaken at the finish line by two other canoes. Joe was bummed—really bummed. He thanked everyone for coming and tried to socialize, but clearly he was under a dark cloud.

I looked at Barb, who sort of shrugged and looked back at me as if to say, *I know, I don't get it either.*

In an attempt to console Joe, I told him not to worry—after all, the second- and third-place winners on *American Idol* usually end up doing much better than the people who come in first.

Why did I say that? I asked myself. *That was the worst analogy in the history of all analogies!*

Poor Joe just nodded politely, looking perplexed. Maybe it was presumptuous of me, but given my recent experiences, I sensed he was a little lost.

Nestor turned to me and, with his back to everyone, made an "L" on his forehead with his fingers so only I could see. I'd made a loser comment for sure, but I was overcompensating because I had a feeling something was up with Joe.

It would've been no revelation to surmise Joe could be suffering from PTSD. The number of soldiers returning from the Middle East wars with PTSD was alarming, and the suicide rates proved it. Joe hadn't been in battle, but as a head and neck surgeon he'd dealt with the brutal aftereffects of gunfire and bombs. But his situation seemed different. I knew he'd loved his time serving in Afghanistan. Once, at our First Communion class at Saint Anthony's, he had told Nestor and me he'd felt incredibly useful at war. Here at home, he appeared uncomfortable in his own skin—like he couldn't quite be present. I didn't know him well enough to conclude much more than that.

After Joe's race, we all agreed to meet at our place later in the afternoon, for one last drink on our beach as the sun went down. I made a few jugs of margaritas, and soon Joe and Barb, Lili and Dewey, Marc and Rikke, and Nestor and I were all sitting on the beach in front of our house, watching the kids and the water as we waited for the sun to go down and the moon to rise. It would have been fun if not for the impending goodbyes and the heaviness that would bring.

Whenever I experience hard goodbyes, I remember my first: at Sydney Airport when I left for America. In those days, the airport had only one lounge and café, where everyone would wait before you boarded. I was shocked so many of my family and friends had shown up, and I wanted to run clear of that café and straight to the gate. I felt sick as I said goodbye to cousins, aunts, uncles, family friends, school friends, and even parents of friends. Every goodbye felt forced as I floated outside of myself and tried to be sunny, fighting back the huge bubbles of tears teetering at the edge of my tear ducts.

The one feeling I couldn't hide came when I said goodbye to my grandfather Pop, who looked fragile and even smaller than his "Leprechaun" nickname implied. Pop was always so positive with me, smiling and laughing as he held me in his strong hug. Saying goodbye to him, I wept. Then, devastated by that goodbye, I stumbled to the gate.

Nine months later, the day before I arrived home, Pop

suddenly died of a stroke. I learned quickly and instinctively the high stakes of leaving, and I've hated goodbyes ever since.

On Kailua Beach that night, even the Cartwrights came down to send us off. They sat and had a drink, telling us they had bought the house and just closed escrow. Hearing the news was a little stab to my heart. They seemed so excited to stay, while I was so sorry to leave. But a few seconds after faking happiness for them, I actually felt it. They looked so peaceful in the pale blue light that fell on the beach right before the moon began to come up out of the ocean. I had a feeling my Kailua had been crowned the winner in their long search for the best place to live. Yay! That made me proud.

Soon it was dark and time to go in. We piled a few bottles of wine and champagne we'd never uncorked, along with some liquor, into the arms of our friends. The kids took the rest of the shells and the boogie boards, and together we all walked outside to say the words I'd been dreading.

We all stood and smiled at each other and then began to hug. I held each of my friends, one by one, and it really hurt— our hugs were tight and long. As I bent down to hug the children, I touched their warm little heads and started to well up. These kids were casual and easy because they knew deep inside they were loved and cared for in all the right ways. Their hugs reminded me of the kind of people their parents are: people who can be relied upon, who place value on matters of the heart.

I was sure I'd see my Hawaiian friends again throughout my life—perhaps not as often as I wanted to, but I'd never let the string get so long it would slacken and drop. They were the kind of friends I needed to hold on to.

❀

By the time we said goodbye to Oʻahu, the *LOST* series finale had aired in America and all around the world. The lead character, Jack, is dying on the island, in real time; the scene is intercut with the secretive church scene Nestor and I had witnessed filming in Honolulu. In this flash sideways to a separate reality, Jack is lured to the vestry, where he sees his dead father, Christian, as a living being. Jack comes to realize why he can see his father: He himself is dead too.

Christian consoles an emotional Jack, encouraging him to go into the chapel, where many of the show's other characters are waiting for him. They are there to help Jack move on. Christian explains that they all created that one place (the chapel) together so when they died, at different times and in different locations, they would have a place to meet. He tells Jack that the most important part of his life was the time he spent with them. And that's why they all needed to be there, so that they could remember their time together and then let go.

This exchange explains many of the show's mysteries. When I watched the scene on television, I also understood why the producers had been so adamant about having everyone there for the filming of it. I suspect they saw the chapel scene as a metaphor for the magical real-life run everyone had on the hit show, and perhaps it was a way to help them all say goodbye and move on as their onscreen counterparts had.

LOST had created some remarkable alchemy and life-changing circumstances for many of the people involved in its production. A good number of the actors had become "big names" and were starting to do big movies with big paychecks. The writers and directors were having no trouble getting work on high-quality shows. The crew, who were mostly locals, had an amazing six-year run of regular work, which is rare for television crews anywhere, let alone in Hawaii. The nature of filmmaking calls for everyone to work together as a true team, like cogs in a wheel. The cast and crew had become 'ohana. They needed that time while shooting the chapel scene to be together and remember what they'd had, so they could say goodbye and start to let go.

I'd caught the tail end of *LOST*'s magical run and somehow managed to fall into a small but wonderful stretch of my own—a condensed time of living without the shadow of myself as an actress. At long last, I'd sunk into who I really was. A huge part of that was the reflection I saw of myself through the eyes of my new friends. Perhaps they were a part of *my* little group who would gather in a church at the end of my days. Perhaps I might be a part of *theirs*.

That last night at our house in Kailua, I lingered outside after watching everyone leave. I needed to look up at the thick covering of stars one last time.

Back inside, Nestor and the boys stood at the entryway, wanting to see if I was okay. Gazing at them, I saw the three most important people in my church, right there beside me, waiting to help me move on.

"Thanks, you guys. I'm fine," I said, hugging them all. "We should get ready for bed."

And that was it. We were in the real world, not the *LOST* world.

How had I built such an otherworldly connection to this Pacific island? As a young person, I'd devoured Austen,

Dickens, and Shakespeare and lived in their world. I'd always thought I'd be at my most comfortable roaming the English countryside. My skin was so pale and prone to sunburn I had to slather on sunblock at least three times a day. But as Lili had once said to me, there are some people who just have Hawaii in their blood.

"And you, my dear," she declared, "are one of those people."

I couldn't imagine ever wanting to leave the rock, but there was no flash sideways in real life—no flash backward or forward in time. We were in the here and now, and we'd always known our stay would have an end. This was the end—the hard, sad end. It was over. Tomorrow we'd be back in Los Angeles.

With that knowledge, I spent my last night listening hard to the dull, steady thud of the small waves on the sand, and the huge, polite slurp as the ocean took the foamy white back to the sea. I tried to memorize those sounds so they'd remain etched in my brain, so I wouldn't forget the privilege of falling asleep to the rhythm of the most beautiful water I'd ever known. I wanted to remember it forever, but it was also time to let it go.

To remember and then let go.

Chapter Nineteen

AUGUST 2010

I wasn't exactly sure how life would be back in Los Angeles. I arrived home almost stripped of my haunting need to be seen as special, as one of the few actresses who had made it big. I felt lightened by my newfound ability to sit in the place I'd landed at the end of my career. And yet a cloud of ache covered me throughout the summer. There was no doubt in my mind I was homesick for Hawaii and Kailua. However, I felt like I was still missing something *inside* of me, like I was lovesick. Missing Kailua felt exactly like losing a love.

I knew the feeling well. I'd lost love all over the place, especially when I was younger.

During my third year of college, when I spent the summer performing Shakespeare up in Santa Cruz, I fell in love with a smart, quirky comic actor who had me laughing from the moment I met him. He was intense and self-effacing—not the Paul Newman to my Joanne Woodward (which was how I'd always pictured my first relationship with an actor) but more the Woody Allen to my Diane Keaton. Fortunately, I was willing to adjust.

I'd been very lonely in America, and that summer was glorious: I performed Shakespeare in a wooded glen while in love with a charismatic guy who loved me back. But by September, it was time to say goodbye. We both had our fourth year of theater school to finish, he in New York and I in Los Angeles. We were dedicated young actors and didn't question our choices for a minute, but I was in no way prepared for the pain that followed.

I was happy and in love, and then I wasn't.

I could touch him and be with him and intuit what he was feeling, and then I couldn't.

Every time I thought about him, I winced. A sharp pain sent throbbing shock waves to my extremities that reverberated back to my heart with an abrupt new sting. I tried to tell myself that my being with him was arbitrary—that I'd needed love only out of loneliness. But that was a lie. I knew he wouldn't be the man I'd marry, but the love we shared was absolute truth, and the end of it was torture.

Now I was feeling the exact same way about Kailua, the town we'd lived in for a year. The intensity of the loss frightened me. It was only a town, for God's sake! But I couldn't fool my broken heart.

About a week after we'd returned home, Nestor had landed a job in Cuetzalan, a small cobblestone-street village in the hills of northern Mexico. The film shoot took him away for five weeks, after which he returned home for just a few days before going up to Vancouver to work on a TV show. He was working hard to provide for our family, and while he felt immense pressure to do so, he also had maid service and someone making his meals—not to mention interesting work to do, with a cast that included Peter O'Toole.

The actress in me wanted to sit with Mr. O'Toole, sip margaritas under the Mexican night sky, and listen to his theater stories for as long as he cared to recount them. But my job now was to settle us all back into our life in LA, so instead I was tasked with establishing the boys in their new routine and playing the roles of chauffeur, cook, cruise director, court jester, and unpacker of a thousand fucking boxes. And gradually, my old resentments resumed with a cookie-cutter sameness that bored even me. Lucky for Nestor, the bad cell reception from that mountain in Mexico made it impossible to unleash any of my unpleasantness on him.

My inability to settle down emotionally and be Nestor's backbone while he was away was so disappointing. In Hawaii, Barb had been ready to give care and consolation to her family at every moment. If she had resentments, at least they hadn't shriveled her up inside. She had shown me the grace that, as Nestor reassured me, I already possessed. I'd found peace in knowing I was enough for us. But back in LA, resentment was clouding my purpose, and it started to hurt again when I breathed.

No one else seemed to miss Hawaii the way I did—not even Rafa, who adored his teacher and became teary at having to say goodbye. The boys were transitioning beautifully. Rafa had started at a morning camp where he enjoyed fencing, making ceramics, and playing basketball. Marco was back at preschool, and they both joined the Burbank Music Academy, where they formed their own little rock band. In Hawaii, they'd spent their downtime exploring the outdoors and the ocean. Perhaps they'd been suffering a little island fever. I could see a lift in their spirits thanks to the wealth of interesting activities available to kids in LA.

Even though I'd arrived home unsure, I knew I'd stripped away much of my ego and the shame I held on to—about never becoming a Famous Actress, working mom, financial contributor, perfect beauty, and mover and shaker all rolled into one. But as I endlessly cut fruit, made sandwiches without crusts, and rescued foam bullets from under the couch, there was Freud muttering in my ear.

Love and work . . .

Work and love . . .

That's all there is, really . . .

I had love, and I had mothering work, but was that enough for me? When I put aside my lovesickness for Kailua, I still felt as though something was missing.

Then August came, Mum and Dad visited, and it was great this time—no "fuck you" fights. Our living room had been piled high with boxes of kitchen supplies waiting to be unpacked into our newly renovated cabinets. One night, after politely stepping through the narrow gaps to get to the TV, Mum softly suggested we start unpacking, saying, "Let's get your lovely new kitchen in order."

"Yes, Bubby," Dad chimed in. "I'll do all the work of the

Tweasies while Nestor is gone." Dad and Nestor had given themselves this nickname years ago, boasting that the odd jobs they did around the house were just "too easy."

The days of their trip to LA ticked by, smoothing over a lot of residual tension from our big fight the previous August in Kailua. My parents helped me so much, instantly becoming the mum and dad I needed. But I realized it wasn't they who'd suddenly become Mum and Dad—it was I who'd become their daughter again. After shedding so much baggage in one short year, I could let them parent me again. Rather than setting myself up to carry their hopes and expectations, I was able to be just their daughter, the mother of their grandchildren, and the wife of the son-in-law whom they adored.

It also confirmed I *had* grown in Hawaii. I'd found my way through the pain of failing at my dream and letting them down. I'd reconciled with who I was in the here and now.

Nestor came home, and Mum and Dad soon said goodbye, but I still felt that lovesick ache for Oʻahu—and the dark cloud that insisted something was missing. Why was I still so emotional? I had come so far. But it was that same darn question: *Is this work enough for me?*

I kept waiting for a sudden revelation, where the mystery would be solved like in a TV show or a play. Should I keep digging? Or should I just give in to life, let the hurt trickle away, and wait for what remained? I wasn't sure what to do.

One day, the four of us were in the car driving through the Valley—a large group of neighborhoods in LA, separated from the LA Basin by the Hollywood Hills. With a deep sigh, I announced that if you squinted really hard, you could sort of pretend the brown hills of Burbank were the Koʻolau Range.

"Wow, babe," said Nestor, "you really have to stop being so cynical about LA."

"Yeah, we love LA," claimed Rafa.

"Yeah, Mama," piped in Marco. "You really are super *cymical*."

I was flabbergasted. Nestor had the audacity to call me cynical? He'd been away all summer in a charming, ancient Mexican village on a frickin' hilltop with Peter O'-bloody-Toole! I felt like my head might actually explode.

I sat in silence in the car, but once we were home, I could no longer hold it in. "I'm so pissed at you," I spat at Nestor.

His shock seemed to be genuine, but that was as far as I got. It was the boys' bedtime—not a moment to steal away and explain.

Rafa and Marco could sense the tension. They knew I was steaming about something, but they had no idea what. Perhaps their little minds subconsciously figured they might as well give me something to *really* be mad at, so they decided to play the "launching game."

I hated the launching game.

They'd invented it with friends over the summer: a one-hun-dred-percent-injury sport that always ended with me mopping up the bloodshed. It was as simple as its name: They'd take turns throwing or "launching" each other as far as they could. As the game began, I quietly began to lose my cool.

Then something flew across the room at lightning speed—so fast my eyes couldn't follow it—and hit me right on the bridge of my nose. It felt like I'd been shot between the eyes.

"Oh my God!" I screamed, covering my face. "What was that?" I stopped breathing for a second. Then the pain really set in, and with it came unstoppable tears. "What was it? What was it?" I cried.

Nestor handed me a hard plastic fish—a barracuda. It looked just like the one that kills Nemo's whole family in the movie. My five-year-old had decided to "launch" the plastic fish at my face.

"Get over there!" Nestor yelled. "You are in a time-out!"

"Did I almost kill Mommy?" Marco cried out from the corner.

This broke my heart and only made me sob more. I wanted to reassure him, but I couldn't stop crying. And it wasn't just the pain.

I was so tired of inadvertently entering their line of fire and being struck by a cushion, a foam bullet, or a plastic disc. And I was so mad at them all for not realizing I was still in grief about having to leave Hawaii.

I felt so alone, so defective. Why was I the only one having trouble readjusting to Hollywood? Every day for the previous eight weeks, I'd thought of Kailua and wished to be back there again—and nobody cared. So I cried some more before Nestor finally led me to our bedroom and shut the door. I lay down on our bed, and I sobbed for a long time.

Eventually, I stopped crying over my anger at them and started to weep for Hawaii.

Perfect images of Kailua flashed through my brain every day— images that were so clear and vivid it was as though I saw them on a liquid mirror that allowed me to reach inside and feel them with my hands. The naupaka shrubs anchored to the sand of the little beach path I walked on multiple times every day. The droplet of seawater I fixed my eye on one day when it fell from my hair, landed on a green pulpy leaf, and bounced into the air before disintegrating into a fleck of mist and light. The strange crack in the mountain I'd study on the way home from school drop-off, leaning over my steering wheel until the traffic light turned green, as I tried to trace its exact depth into the crevice beneath it. Images like these were constantly transporting me back to Hawaii.

Lying on my bed, I wept for it all.

I wept for the minutes that seemed stretched and my exhales that felt longer. I wept for the ease with which Nestor and I could convince each other to play hooky on those days when the Kailua ocean had flattened and the water was so clear you could spot the tiniest goby shuffling by on the sandy seafloor. I wept for the way Nestor would suddenly spring up from his beach chair, mid-conversation, and race into the water so he could swim alongside a sea turtle he'd spotted from the shore. I wept for our new friends' faces, open and sun-kissed, and for their children's glowing orange pumpkins bobbing haphazardly in the dark grey air on Halloween night. I wept for the happiness of coming home and seeing familiar cars parked in our driveway, ready for a beach day.

I wept for chairs dug in the sand and relaxed conversations as eyes gazed out to sea . . . for kids building sand walls, riding boogie boards, and catching rare Spanish Dancer slugs and crabs in buckets . . . for jumpy, sandy feet waiting to be hosed down. I wept for how easy it was to know those people and how hard it was to leave them.

I wept for our Kailua house and the rattling wind that made it feel so alive. I wept for the North Shore, our Eastern Shore, and the lush forest interior where we hiked through paradise. I wept for Waikiki, where we shared so many meals with loved ones while sipping the best Mai Tai cocktails on the planet.

And then I wept for the gifts only God could have given us that year: the rainbow that planted itself evenly over our back-yard just as the kids came out to play, the ibis that flew with Rafa and me while we were riding bikes, the steeple from Saint Anthony's that surprised me on my beach walk, the clouds that rose like a golden halo over the Koʻolau mountains when I stopped atop Lanikai headland.

In that tiny place on earth, for a short time and with a handful of people, some magic potion had washed over me and brought healing. Now, my tears told me, I was hanging on so tightly to that magic—to the memory of Hawaii—because I was frightened.

I didn't have all the answers yet. A part of me wasn't right, and I needed to know why. I wasn't sure I could remember and let go—like Jack's father, Christian, had told him to do. What if I let go . . . and then I forgot? The magic potion might wear off, and I'd be left with nothing. I'd be back where I started: a lost person.

As I began to feel sleepy, I promised myself that I wouldn't let go of Hawaii yet—that the answer would come soon, and I'd feel whole.

Don't let go, don't let go, I repeated to myself. *You don't need to move on just yet.*

But it was getting harder and harder to stay awake, so I chanted some more.

Remember it all, remember it all. But don't *let go . . .*

Then somewhere in the middle of trying not to forget, trying not to let go, and trying not to fall asleep, I let go . . . and I slept.

Chapter Twenty

AUGUST 2010

I awoke the next day much the same way I'd been waking up since leaving O'ahu: with my mind on the island. I hadn't let go, and I hadn't forgotten. Only this morning, I was thinking about one person in particular: Joe, and our discussion that time at Saint Anthony's.

Nestor and I were in our First Communion parenting class one Sunday toward the end of our stay, when Barb wasn't in class and Joe had been back from Afghanistan only about three or four weeks. Seated between Nestor and Joe in a small classroom next to the church, I bowed my head when the priest asked us to pray.

Public prayer on demand has never really worked for me. I spend too much time on the niceties.

Hello, God. How are you?
Hope you're well.

Everything here is fine.

I needed to work my way into an intimate dialogue with God, but just as I'd be getting there, the prayer time would inevitably be over.

Joe, however, didn't seem to have this problem—at least not on that day. As soon as he bowed his head, he seemed to be engaged in some internal struggle. His prayer looked like a plea to God.

I admired the way Joe prayed so openly and soulfully. It was brave. It wasn't hard to see he was a good man and extremely intelligent. It seemed his mind was rarely quiet. Today, I thought perhaps he was feeling some kind of obligation—and maybe some guilt at not being able to meet it.

As we made our way out of the class, I curbed my instinct to ask if Joe was okay. While we walked, however, he took the opportunity to open up to Nestor and me. Lying in my bed back in LA months later, I tried to recall his exact words.

Joe had shaken his head and laughed, then lowered his eyes and spoke—abstractly at first, as though he were trying to unravel something that was confounding him. Then he had taken a breath and started to speak frankly about his time on the base in Bagram and how useful he'd felt in the operating theater. He'd said that he felt a need to go back, that he *wanted* to go back. He'd shared some stories about the OR and how it was kind of like the Wild West—stressful at times—but his eyes had lit up, and it was easy to see he'd felt good over there. Looking at him now, I wondered if he was feeling guilty about yearning to be back in Afghanistan.

Nestor wondered if Joe might have felt guilty about abandoning his brothers at war. "Many soldiers re-enlist because they feel bad leaving their guys behind," he suggested to me that day. Joe had gone to West Point, and the military had put him through med school. Perhaps it is an awful irony: to want peace yet feel you are functioning at your best during a time of war.

I, on the other hand, took Joe to mean that he felt bad about Barb and the kids—about leaving them to fend for themselves and worry about his well-being for almost a year while he'd found a place where he'd been at the top of his game.

Months later, on that morning in LA, as this was all running through my mind, I had an epiphany.

Those months in Afghanistan may have changed Joe irreversibly. Perhaps he wanted to bring home the person he'd become over there, but he was somehow unable to do that. And while I could hardly compare myself to Joe—a man who'd been laboring in service of his country and in the hopes of making the world a safer place—I could relate.

I was working in service of two boys and, to a lesser degree, my husband, and I too had made an internal shift and found a place in time when I was at my best. While in Hawaii, I'd reconciled with who I was after giving up on my dream, and I wanted to bring that woman back home to LA. But my adventure was over, and I didn't know how to put my new self into action in my regular life. Much like the survivors on *LOST* who yearned to be back on the island, I yearned to go back to Hawaii, to the place where I'd won the battle with my ego— the place where I was the happiest I'd ever been. But going back was impossible.

Armed with the knowledge of that impossibility, I pulled myself out of bed and pushed Hawaii out of my mind.

There is a scene in *LOST* where John Locke finds Sun—the wife of Daniel Dae Kim's Jin—angrily searching in the dirt for her missing wedding ring. When John reveals he used to be angry all the time, Sun claims she can't remember ever seeing him angry and asks why he is no longer that way. John explains it's because he's not lost anymore. Sun asks him how he managed to do that, to which John responds he found what was lost because he stopped looking.

And that's exactly what happened to me.

Rafa was about to start back at his old elementary school in LA, so we needed to stock him up with supplies for third grade. I'd finally put our renovated kitchen back in order, but I hadn't yet unpacked the school supplies. So, heading out to our freestanding garage, I waded through the piles of old furniture, some broken-down exercise equipment, and filthy stacks of framed photographs that had been carelessly covered by some ripped sheets. About halfway to the back of the garage, I came across a trio of cardboard moving boxes.

I froze.

I knew immediately what those boxes were. I'd been hauling them around for years.

Crouching down, I read the labels: *Shannon's Acting Journals*. My heart rate increased, and a wave of heat flushed over me. Something in me suddenly needed to look at my old journals.

The white lid on the top box was now almost black with a thick layer of greasy dust and dirt—that oily consistency LA outdoor dust always seems to settle into. Careful not to stick my fingers into the side holes of the boxes lest I be bitten by one of the hundreds of black widows inhabiting our garage, I kicked the top two boxes to the ground. Then I pushed all three of them with my feet, past the garage door.

Out in the sunlight, I kicked off the lids and gave each box a vigorous shake, jumping away quickly to give the spiders some space to escape. But none appeared. Looking up at me were dozens of old notebooks of all shapes and sizes and a bunch of black-and-white composition books I used toward the end of my acting career.

My heart pounding, I pulled the journals out of the boxes as though I were reading love letters from a man I'd never gotten over. And opening them one by one, I began to read.

The books were filled with stories—the backstories of most of the characters I'd played during and after college, and even some I'd merely auditioned for. That was how I worked. Guided by the script, I made up the history of the woman I was playing. If the script had a line or an action that carried behind it some aspect of the person's past life, I wrote about it.

In some cases there were multiple journals devoted to just one character's life, like Ibsen's Hilde in *The Master Builder*. Her motives are nuanced, and Ibsen is vague about whether or not her intentions are good or bad. Layered and full of contradictions, Hilde required that I play her every action with a specific motivation informed by her past. For me, the only way to walk the delicate balancing act of that character was to create her whole backstory in a detailed way. Writing it all down helped the character travel from pen to paper and into my body.

Other roles required shorter backstories (just a few pages), like George's girlfriend Alison on the sitcom *Seinfeld*.

The role was small and pretty straightforward. Still, the history I wrote became the portal into the mind and soul of the person I was playing.

Holding those journals in my driveway, I felt something sublime, so much so that I pulled the books close to my heart. Just touching them electrified a part of me that had dulled since I'd walked away from acting. I could feel it. When I pushed the books away from me, the charge petered out; I pulled them closer and it sparked up again. I knew right then and there that I'd found something profound: an invaluable piece of my puzzle.

I ended up bringing all three boxes to my bedroom. I'd fallen in love with the characters I'd played over the course of my career, but I thought I'd said goodbye to them when the productions were over. And yet here they were, still alive in those pages. As I read through my notebooks, I time-traveled to the moments when I was most alive as an actor and sometimes even as a human being. But I'd walked away from the performer in me, the industry had changed, only a few shows shot in LA, and there was no way we could both work at the same time. I wasn't sure I could go back now, even if I wanted to.

So what was the pull? Why were these pages waking up some sleeping part of me? Because I still loved the stories—the ones I was able to help tell and those I'd created for my women.

On my bedroom floor beside the boxes, under a tall stack of other journals, gleamed the gold leather-bound notebook my LA girlfriends had gifted me before I traveled to Hawaii. By the time we left Kailua, that golden notebook had become the foundation of that small tower of diaries. And that's when I decided to start reading *my own* story of that year.

I read a little every day. Then I wrote more as I remembered the rich details of our family's journey on the island. It took some time, but I began to see how writing, especially, had been a huge part of my creative process over the years.

If the act of putting the words onto paper was a channel through which I was able to find the character's heart and motivation, to better serve the writer's story, then why couldn't I do the opposite? Why not put words onto paper and find the heart of a story *I* wanted to tell—and let it live *outside* of me?

So that's what I started to do. And as I wrote, I stumbled upon the heart of my diaries, and all the many revelations Hawaii had provided.

I'd realized that by going to Mass every week, I could restore my faith in God and find that strong anchor I'd lost since Prayer Hill.

I'd grown to understand that my yearning to relive my teenage years was misguided—that I really had no desire to travel back to that time when my singular purpose was to find romantic love. Rather, I longed for the sweet freedom of a life uncluttered by heady expectations of how to be significant. And I'd discovered that in the end, all I really needed from those years was to accept them as my bright and shining memories. And most of all, I finally realized I had found exactly what I was searching for back then: someone to love romantically, soulfully, who loved me back.

I'd come to accept myself as a mother and a wife—as the woman I was *now*, who had fallen into that role, and as the little girl I'd been long ago, who had never played with dollhouses or ever dreamed of becoming a homemaker. I'd realized it was okay to treasure my family above all else, even though at times my instinct was to break free of it all, like a bird escaping her cage.

I'd learned that I needed to accept the mistakes of my parents just as I hoped my kids would accept mine—and that the love I have for my mum and dad is so all-encompassing it's embedded in every cell in my body.

And I was coming to grips with the new me—without the drive of my career, without the added label of Famous Actress.

But there was one thing I hadn't learned in Hawaii, something that hadn't occurred to me to address at any time since I walked away from acting: the loss of myself as a creative being.

One of my best friends, Adelaide, is the person I know in this world whose heart is surrounded by the least amount of noise. She never seems to need directions to the truth. Whenever we talk about how she gave up her acting career to raise five children, she says, "I'm just slowly dying inside," and not much more. I've always marveled at her openness, yet I never fully understood what she was saying. She's a happy wife and friend who is always up for a good time or a meaningful conversation, and she mothers her kids with an artful balance of joyful appreciation and sensible expectations. But after those days poring through the notebooks from my garage, her words came back to me and hit me hard, like Marco's fish in my face. I'd never stopped to think that walking away from acting also meant the end of my creative self, and that end—that slow death—was causing great pain. It was making me feel lost.

Upon leaving acting, I had decided to go to war with my twelve-year-old self, the one who wrote the vow:

SHANNON KENNY WILL BE A
FAMOUS ACTRESS

Entrenched in my new job as "just" a wife and mom, I'd hated that twelve-year-old's superficial need to be singled out, to be crowned special and worthwhile, to fly as far away from normal as she could get. It was only after my discovery in the garage that I realized the many gifts she had given me.

In that string of small beach towns where I grew up, a career in the arts was not the norm. Most of my friends from childhood became shipwrights and secretaries, nurses and real estate agents. My quest for fame was an excuse to make up plays, to pretend long past the appropriate age, and to live inside my make-believe worlds.

That youthful make-believer helped me travel over an ocean to learn my craft, which I did with reverence, duty bound at all costs to play my roles with authenticity and truth and to always aid in telling the greater story.

The goal of my twelve-year-old self had been fame, but somewhere along the line she allowed me to become an actress. And as a woman now, I saw this had been a worthy goal to pursue at all costs. And so I let that girl back in, with no purpose other than to avoid destroying all that she had made for me.

The next time we visited Australia, I searched for my old cedar chest in my parents' basement. When I found it, the box that held my vow was still there. I'd neatly printed the word "private" in miniscule letters on the upper left-hand corner of the lid. The note was still folded up inside.

I pulled out the piece of newspaper; it was from *The Sun* on April 30, 1981. I'd scrawled those words in red nail polish, just as I'd remembered.

I brought the little box with the note inside it back to America with me and placed it in a drawer in my bedroom. It still sits there today. It acts as my permission slip, allowing me to keep my creative self alive. And I have done just that, and I continue to do it. Feeding my creativity was the final lesson I needed to learn in what had become a long journey home.

Slowly and steadily, I've managed to fill the hole in my chest. I live with the knowledge that of course I will have more holes punched in me again—after all, "love is God's mistake."

I was a lost person—and then my amazing adventure on the *LOST* island, the most meaningful land I've ever known, helped me gain precious clarity. From a new perspective, I'm able to look back on my life and see it is beautiful—and beautifully awful as well. I deeply understand now what I imagined Freud had been whispering in my ear: "Love and work . . . work and love, that's all there is."

I agree, Dr. Freud. I cannot live on love alone. I need more. I need to work at keeping my creative self in action.

Though I walked away from my dreams of acting, I am still a creative being as much as I am a wife, a mother, a daughter, a sister, and a friend. The shift inside has brought me to a place where I am able to let it all back in.

And I am not lost anymore.

ACKNOWLEDGMENTS

Jennie Nash, thank you for teaching with such clarity. Thank you for your honesty, your patience, your generosity, your good humor, your kindness, your encouragement, your advocacy, your push, and your friendship.

My heartfelt thanks to you, Joannie Burstein. You were as supportive and excited about this book as you were about me when I met you fresh out of theater school. I am so grateful to have had you by my side all of these years.

To everyone at Greenleaf Book Group, especially Justin Branch, Jen Glynn, Jessica Choi, Kirstin Andrews, Amanda Hughes, Corrin Foster, and Kristine Peyre-Ferry, thank you for your across-the-board kindness and excellence.

Thank you to Amy Dorta McIlwaine for a smooth and insightful editing experience. I learned so much. It was a pleasure.

Cameron Stein, I love the cover of this book. Thank you for making this process a collaborative one. You are a big talent and so understated. You will do so well.

To every single person who worked on *LOST*, I want to thank you as a fan for giving me the gift of a weekly escape, for your wondrous stories that piqued my curiosity and left me wanting more. I especially want to thank you, Carlton Cuse, for your unending kindness to my family and for your advice and encouragement with regard to this book.

To my girlfriends, my kindred spirits, my inspirations, my joy, my places to fall, I thank you all for your friendship and your unending support.

Alison Bley, Nina Coleman, Mieke Holkeboer, Jenny Riley, Katrina Vrenegor, Dianne Ventresca, Cameron Thieriot, Joel Delman and Tarina Tarantino, thank you for your early reads, generous feedback, and help.

To my friends who allowed me to write about them, Barb, Joe, Joey, Lili, Dewey, Irene, Scot, Rike, Marc, Annie, Ian, Angel, Jayne, Kerrie, Jenny, Joannie, Dianne and Vincent, thank you for your open minds and creative spirits and for your trust in me.

For Mum, Dad, and Sean, thank you for your bravery and for trusting that our light far outweighs our dark because our light is love, and the amount of love I have for you makes any bump absolutely surmountable.

To Rafa and Marco, thank you for your selflessness while I worked on this book and for your support. Thank you for being both kind and good. You are my heart.

And finally, thank you, Nestor. Thank you for being my partner and my love. You are everything that's true.

ABOUT
THE AUTHOR

Shannon Kenny Carbonell grew up in Sydney, Australia, and moved to the US at age 18 to study acting. After earning a BFA in Theater from the California Institute of the Arts (CalArts), she worked in regional theater, where she had the privilege of playing some classic roles like Nina in *The Seagull*, Julie in *Miss Julie*, and Helena in *A Midsummer Night's Dream*.

She then transitioned into television guest star roles, one of her favorites being Katrina Banks on HBO's *Dream On*—a parody of Courtney Love—where she got to shoot heroin between her toes, sing in a music video with Brian Benben, and (being the *excitable girl* she was) experience the thrill of meeting Warren Zevon. Her other favorite guest star role was playing Allison, George's girlfriend, on NBC's *Seinfeld*; it was her favorite because, well . . . it was *Seinfeld*.

Shannon was cast in series regular roles on TV shows and,

if she fails to rank the show, *Muscle*, as her best experience, she'd risk offending her wonderful husband Nestor; it was on this show that the two of them defied producers' orders not to date other cast members. Shannon also played leads in TV movies and mini-series, working opposite acting legends like James Garner and Sam Shepard.

Additionally, she voiced scores of cartoon characters. One of Shannon's most memorable offers came by way of the animated series, *The Wild Thornberrys*, where she was cast specifically because of her Australian accent. Upon arriving at the sound stage, Shannon discovered that her role would simply involve her barking like a dog—albeit an Australian dingo.

Shannon lives in Los Angeles with her husband Nestor, their two sons Rafa and Marco, and their dog Donna Borrelli Carbonell.

All in Not LOST is her first book.